FREIGHT TRAIN CARS

Mike Schafer with Mike McBride

MBI Publishing Company

First published in 1999 by MBI Publishing Company, 729 Prospect Avenue, PO Box 1, Osceola, WI 54020-0001 USA

MBI Publishing Company books are also available at discounts in bulk quantity for industrial or sales-promotional use. For details write to Special Sales Manager at Motorbooks International Wholesalers & Distributors, 729 Prospect Avenue, Osceola, WI 54020-0001 USA.

Library of Congress Cataloging-in-Publication Data Available
ISBN 0-7603-0612-5

On the front cover: Helping feed the nation, covered grain hoppers congregate with other types of freight cars at the Union Pacific yard in Columbus, Nebraska, in September 1998. Once the domain of the once-ubiquitous boxcar, covered hoppers now reign as one of the most common types of freight cars found on U.S. railroads. *Howard Ande*

On the frontispiece: The handbrake of a Santa Fe boxcar. Although all modern freight cars are equipped with automatic brakes, they must also be equipped with a set of manual brakes. Like an automobile's parking brake, the manual handbrake of a railcar is applied when the car is parked. *Steve Smedley*

On the title page: Loaded coal gondolas string out across a Texas sunset near Brenham in 1996. *Tom Kline*

On the back cover: Loaded with soybeans, colorful covered hoppers of the Ann Arbor Railroad stand at Oak Grove, Michigan, in April 1982. Unfortunately, their journey to market has been briefly interrupted by a minor derailment, and the cars must await attention by railroad crews for rerailing. *Forrest L. Becht*

Edited by Jack Savage
Designed by Katie L. Sonmor

Printed in Hong Kong

CONTENTS

ACKNOWLEDGMENTS

For many readers of this book, the acknowledgment page will be among the first you'll read. But for authors, it's usually the last thing we write. At this point, the project is about to be a "wrap." The work has been but a blur (you know how deadlines are!), but as things settle back down, it becomes clearer to us just how many people lent their help in making *Freight Cars* possible.

I'll start with my co-author and right-hand man on this project, Mike McBride. I first met Mike in 1964 when both of us were just getting into documenting railroad history through photography, and we've been doing that as friends ever since. I've long known of Mike's interest in freight cars, so he was my first choice as co-author of this book.

Four outside contributors deserve special applause: Forrest Becht, Gerald A. Hook, Tom Kline, and Mike Del Vecchio. Forrest submitted an impressive and well-organized array of freight-car photography—enough for a 200-page book of just his material. Likewise, Gerald Hook submitted an extensive selection of photo material and helpful resource material. Tom Kline proved that there are a lot more people out there photographing freight cars than you might imagine, and when it came to early, exotic freight-car photos, Mike Del Vecchio proved his capabilities as a true freight-car historian. And to Chuck Yungkurth, a longtime freight-car historian and technical artist, we thank you for your help in double-checking the manuscript for errors and inconsistencies.

We'd also like to thank the Milwaukee Road Historical Association for letting us delve into their photo archives for additional early photos. Thank-yous also go out to Dave Oroszi, Brad McClelland, Steve Smedley, Howard Ande, Ted Schnepf, Greg Heier, John Dziobko, Alvin Smith, Bob Penisi, Jim Boyd, James Mischke, Sam Caliciotti, and the late Hank Goerke for photo contributions.

For all his support (and horsewhipping to keep us on schedule with this project), I'd like to thank Steve Esposito, my friend and associate within our company, Andover Junction Publications. And, in closing, a tip of the hat must go to the folks at MBI Publishing for turning this project into a product that we hope readers will find informative and entertaining.

—*Mike Schafer*

Reading slogans and railroad heralds has long been a tradition for folks waiting trackside for a train to pass. Two words, "Everywhere West," told observers in a nutshell where the Chicago, Burlington & Quincy went. *Mike McBride*

"Expressway for Industry" proclaims the Detroit & Toledo Shore Line boxcar standing at the Shore Line's Lang Yard at Toledo, Ohio, in 1964. The slogan played upon truck competition but in the coming years, boxcars like this that were once a familiar sight all over America would yield to truck trailers and new breeds of freight cars. *Hank Goerke*

7

1   Evolution of the Freight Car

Like just about everything else on planet Earth, the railroad freight car evolved from naively simple beginnings. And some have changed more than others. In some respects, flatcars aren't very much different than they were in 1850, but check out today's fancy mechanical refrigerator cars—they're bigger and more sophisticated than a whole nineteenth-century general store.

The First Freight Car

The American freight car traces its roots to England. Early railroads in England attempted to operate like turnpikes—anyone could take their horse and wagon on the tracks. This soon proved unfeasible, and locomotives began hauling privately owned "wagons"— an arrangement (and nomenclature) that lasted until recent times.

In America, the freight car—such as it then was— preceded the first chartered railroads, first appearing in the early 1820s on rudimentary railways or similar fixed-guideway transport systems within industrial endeavors such as coal mines or stone quarries. English influence in America was strong, even after the Revolutionary War, so these operations incorporated cars designed like their English brethren, which were basically oversize wagons. The newfangled railcars became preferred over horse-hauled wagons on roadways because—especially hooked together as a train—they were easier to move and could carry more.

The first railway large enough to be considered a commercial operation unto itself (and possibly among the first to have its own name) is acknowledged by

Freight cars are everywhere in the scene at Dixon, Illinois, during the summer of 1973. An Illinois Central freight bound from Freeport to Clinton, Illinois, is passing under the Chicago & North Western's Chicago-Omaha main line over which another freight is rolling. America's food and goods are on the move. *Mike McBride*

A replica of the forerunner of the modern gondola—a "flour car" belonging to the Baltimore & Ohio Railroad—is shown in 1956 mounted on a flatcar for a special railroad-sponsored display in New Jersey. The replica represents a four-wheel car from 1832 that was used to haul barrels of flour on B&O's pioneering 13-mile line from Ellicott Mills to Baltimore, Maryland. *John Dziobko*

many transportation historians to be the Granite Railway at Quincy, Massachusetts, a private operation opened in 1826. This five-foot-gauge, two-mile-long line was used to transport cut stone blocks and slabs—some weighing up to 65 tons—between the quarry and riverboat transportation. To carry out this task, the railway employed horse-drawn timber platforms on wheels—a flatcar, if you will.

In 1827 in the coal fields of eastern Pennsylvania, the Lehigh Coal & Navigation Company began moving coal from mountaintop mines down to riverboats by way of a nine-mile gravity railway. Coal loaded into crude "jimmies"—the precursor to the hopper car—was sent, in trains of up to 14 cars, zig-zagging down the gently sloped line with a brakeman controlling the speed. (By 1829, the line was carrying passengers, purely for entertainment, and is considered the birthplace of the American roller coaster. The Mauch Chunk Switchback Railway, as it later became known, operated until 1938.)

Obviously, by the mid-1820s, some folks had begun to realize the potential of the railway as a fast and economical means of moving large amounts of bulk commodities in all kinds of weather—which is what American railroads still do best. Bigger things had begun to happen. The year 1826 had seen the birth of the Mohawk & Hudson Railroad in Upstate New York, the first chartered (that is, authorized by a governing body) railroad to be built in America. In 1827, the Baltimore & Ohio was born as America's first "common-carrier"—that is, a transportation company expressly for public use. Roadways had long been established by this time, and canals were also a popular mode, the famous Erie Canal having been completed between Albany and Buffalo in 1825. But "fast" and "all-weather" descriptions did not apply to these modes at the time—and never would for the canal—and as mid-century approached, the railway was on a roll.

Though the very earliest rail operations were built to move freight, rail quickly became popular for passenger transport once chartered railroads began proliferating. The trains of the pioneer railroads such as B&O often carried both freight and passengers at the same time. Passengers rode in either crude, wagonlike cars or in what were essentially stagecoaches on flanged wheels. The flatcar and especially the gondola (a flatcar with sides) initially were the conveyances of choice for freight, much of which was carried in crates and barrels, although coal and such could be dumped directly into gondolas.

With rare exceptions, these early cars rode on rigid, two-axle wheel assemblies attached directly to the car. Early on, railroads learned that some sort of springing system between wheels and carbody was necessary to reduce the jarring effect of a ride over then-crude track. Not only did wheel springs reduce damage to freight and discomfort to passengers, they lengthened the life of the carbody itself. By the mid-1830s, sprung wheels were widely embraced.

Into the 1830s, American railway technology still reflected that of its mother country, England. If American railways of the period didn't actually order cars and locomotives from English manufacturers, they at least built them to English design—primarily to standards set forth by George Stephenson and his son, Robert, of the Liverpool & Manchester Railway.

There came a point, however, where American practice began deviating from English standards, in part because of clearances. In the civilized, settled land of England, railways were quick to adopt high-level station platforms, which allowed passengers to board cars without having to climb steps. The downside was that high-level station platforms and the overhead walkways that connected them restricted the width of locomotives and rolling stock. These clearance restrictions would affect numerous foreign railways, especially those of the British, for decades. Even today, the locomotives and rolling stock of foreign railways seem more diminutive than American equipment—even on railways that share the nearly worldwide standard track gauge of 4 feet, 8-1/2 inches.

Newly proliferating American railroads weren't hampered by such formalities as high-level station platforms. Rather, passengers hiked on board from ground-level platforms. What does this have to do with freight cars? The lack of serious clearance restrictions allowed American railways to build ever-larger locomotives and rolling stock—passenger and freight. English designs could be amplified, and cars became larger and heavier.

Another particularly radical departure from English practice was the enclosed freight car. In England, where rail routes were relatively short, year-round mild weather was the rule, coke-fired steam locomotives burned clean, and flatcars and gondolas were more than adequate for freight transport. In America, vicious winter weather, baking-hot summer sun, long treks between settled areas, and soft-coal-fired locomotives spewing cinders prompted a more protective means of freight conveyance, and early in the 1830s—Presto!—the covered gondola was born. From this evolved the boxcar, destined to become an icon of American freight railroading.

About the same time, American freight-car design made another abrupt departure from English practice with the development of two-truck cars. Rigid, four-wheel cars did not perform well on American track,

Save for the wheels and truck assemblies and minor appliances such as brake wheels and truss rods, Chicago, Milwaukee & St. Paul boxcar No. 20851 is an all-wood car being rolled out of Milwaukee Shops in 1891. Regardless, the era of all-wood freight and passenger cars is drawing to an end; by this time carbuilders were using an increased number of metal components. By the turn of the century, all-steel construction would be proving itself. *Rails Unlimited, Ted Schnepf collection*

Although flatcars and gondolas on early American railroads had their roots in England, the boxcar appears to be an American phenomenon, developed as a means of protecting a car's contents not only from harsh weather but from locomotive cinders. Eventually the boxcar would rise to become that jack-of-all-trades of freight conveyance. *Mike Del Vecchio collection*

which often had been rapidly and crudely constructed. By their nature, four-wheel cars had to be short lest they bind on curves. Further, since the weight of the car and its cargo was concentrated on just four wheels, that weight was transferred to a short section of track, making the brittle iron rail more vulnerable to breakage. The high weight-per-wheel ratio also led to a greater incidence of overheated wheel bearings and broken axles.

The solution to these problems was the two-truck, eight-wheel car. The identity of the inventor(s) of the double-truck freight car has been lost to antiquity, but the Baltimore & Ohio Railroad appears to have been one of the pioneers of two-truck, freight-car operation in the early 1830s.

Two-truck, eight-wheel cars—with each four-wheel truck independently sprung and able to swivel freely on a "bolster" that supported the carbody—spread the weight and permitted longer cars. Double-trucked cars showed a remarkable ability to negotiate curving and uneven trackage. By the late 1830s, double-trucked cars were being heavily promoted, and almost overnight they became widely accepted by nearly all railroads except for a few holdouts in New England that continued to use four-wheel cars almost universally until about 1870. The irony of today's railroading is that four-wheel cars have made a comeback, albeit limited, in the form of four-wheel "spine" cars used for hauling single truck trailers.

Freight-Car Development Accelerates

By the mid-1800s, rail had become the superior form of transportation for passengers and freight. Railroads were being built as fast as humanly possible, and they were being used to carry anything that needed to be transported—regardless of size, weight, or makeup, be it solid, liquid, or powder, mineral or organic. This diversity of commodities prompted shippers to demand freight-car designs that were more tailored to their needs. Although the ever-frugal railroads would have preferred to handle all freight with a fleet of just a couple types of cars—mainly gondolas and flatcars—new car types did emerge: the boxcar, the covered gondola, the stockcar, the reefer, the tank car, the auto-rack, and so on right up to the relatively recent introduction of the articulated (jointed) stack or well car. The evolution of each of these car types is covered in more detail in the following chapters.

Uninhibited by the clearance restrictions that plague British railways to this day, American railroads began employing ever-larger rolling stock after the Civil War. From the time of the introduction of double-trucked cars in the late 1830s through the war, car capacity had stagnated at about 10 tons or less, with average length at about 25 feet. The postwar boom prompted carbuilders to redesign cars with increased capacities, pushing the envelope to 15 tons, then to 20, and so on until 40-ton-capacity cars became widespread in the infant years of the twentieth century.

What's in a Number
(and all those other markings on the side of a freight car)?

The markings on the side of a typical freight car are a treasure chest of information. The purpose of some of those markings is obvious; others are not. Here's how to "read" a freight car:

Owner's name and/or logo: Usually the most prominent marking on a freight car is the name and/or herald of its operator (which is not always necessarily the car's owner). The owner's popular name is sometimes spelled out, billboard style, or sometimes only the initials are given.

Reporting marks: These markings are of prime importance not only to the clerks who must keep track of cars, but to train conductors who are shepherding a car through its journey. The reporting marks consist of the owner's initials in its most condensed form, along with the car's number. Often, the initials will contain an "X", signifying that the car had owners other than a railroad company. Also, the car owner may have more than one set of reporting marks, although only one can be used per car. For example, SFRA, SFRP, and SFRD were all used by the Atchison, Topeka & Santa Fe.

Light weight (LT. WT.) is the unloaded weight of the car in multiples of 100 pounds. Cars are weighed when new and re-weighed periodically thereafter, or when repairs or modifications change the weight.

Load limit (LD. LMT.) is the maximum permissible weight of contents, including the lading itself, dunnage (pallets, bracing, packing material), and temporary fixtures (ice, fuel, etc.). The load limit is determined by subtracting the light weight from the total weight.

Mike Schafer

Capacity (CAPY.) is the nominal weight of lading the car is rated for, in multiples of 1,000 pounds.

The new date (NEW) indicates when the car was weighed new to find its light weight.

The built date (BLT) indicates when the car was built.

Plate C notation (EXCEEDS PLATE C): Plate C is an AAR (Association of American Railroads) diagram that outlines the maximum size a car can be for clearance on most railroad lines. A car that exceeds these dimensions must be stenciled "Exceeds Plate C", and thus would be restricted from general interchange service because it might not clear certain bridges or other structures on some roads.

The car number (as part of the reporting marks) itself can also tell a story. Why are cars numbered in the first place? Railroads assign numbers to locomotives, freight and passenger cars, track-construction machinery, and virtually everything else as part of the system for keeping track of everything from an item's purchase date to its current location. Often, railroads assign a particular number series to different types of cars. On the Chicago & North Western Railway, for example, 4000-series numbers were assigned to general-service 40-foot boxcars with 6-foot doors; a 25000-series number indicated a 40-foot boxcar with an 8-foot door suitable for clean lading (like canned food); 60000-series numbers were assigned to three-dump hoppers. All of these numbering nuances are useful and necessary for car accounting and car marshaling. Each railroad's car roster is listed in *The Official Railway Equipment Register* along with other information such as car type, dimensions, capacity, and size of doors.

For a country obsessed with growth and the subsequent need for transportation, larger cars were a natural. In terms of the tonnage they could haul, bigger cars represented less capital expenditure per ton-mile (a ton of cargo hauled one mile)—certainly an important consideration for railroads. A given amount of freight could be handled with fewer cars, and fewer cars meant less clogging of yards. "Bigger is better" became (and remains) the accepted freight-car format.

Construction

Throughout the nineteenth century, wood was the construction material of choice because of its abundance (which also made it cheap) and ease of fabrication. Metalworking was still in its infancy at the end of that century. Although certain car parts, such as wheels and couplers, had to be iron, just about everything else was wood, even the center sill—the car's "spine."

Early cars were little more than flat platforms or simple framed boxes on wheels, which did not make them particularly durable in the stressful environment of being shoved or pulled, along with other cars, by a locomotive. Early on, builders quickly learned that a carbody constructed around an underframe comprising a center sill(s), with body bolsters for added strength and rigidity, was far better. This was about as radical a change in car-design philosophy that ever came along, for railroads and carbuilders were hesitant to explore any design deviations that weren't already tried and proven. After all, railroads needed cars for plain and simple transportation; they weren't in the business of innovative freight-car technology. Besides, there was no time for radical innovation. So many freight cars were needed by the booming railroad industry that cars by necessity had to be cheap, and the way to keep them cheap was to build them using those tried-and-proven methods with abundantly available material—wood.

One radical change in freight-car technology can trace its roots to 1845 when one of the richest and largest concentrations of iron ore in the world was discovered surrounding Lake Superior in what are today the states of Minnesota, Wisconsin, and (upper) Michigan. In the few years following this discovery, there emerged a process by which pig iron could be transformed inexpensively into large quantities of steel, a

Although the all-steel car had proven itself well by World War I, many "composite" cars (metal and wood) were still being constructed, such as this Northwestern Pacific boxcar being switched at a Pacific Lumber Company facility circa 1940. This World War I-era car features steel ends, center sill, and framing, but the framing is sandwiched (and therefore hidden from view) between wood side sheathing, inside and out. *Southern Pacific, Mike Del Vecchio collection*

metal that possessed greater strength, lighter weight, and more malleability than iron. Steel would revolutionize railcar construction, to say little of American industry in general.

Representing America's first major steel-construction project was the 1874 opening of the Eads Bridge, a rail/roadway span over the Mississippi River at St. Louis. Once the refinements of steel-making became widely embraced as the century closed, new steel-making complexes arose along Great Lakes shores near Chicago and Cleveland. Iron ore was moved in (wooden) freight cars from mines to Lake Superior docks for transshipment to Great Lakes boats for transport to the new steel plants. Likewise, the new mills were fueled by coal and coke brought in from the East by rail in (wooden) gondolas and hoppers. Steel was rebuilding America—and eventually its railroads.

Railroads quickly accepted steel as a superior substitute for iron rails, but not so for car construction. Iron rails were brittle and prone to breakage (thanks in part to unduly heavy locomotives made of iron), which resulted in spectacular, expensive train wrecks. Though lighter than equivalent volumes of iron, steel rail was much tougher and allowed for larger locomotives and rolling stock—and for locomotives to be larger, steel construction was mandatory to reduce weight and yet increase strength.

America's ever-conservative railroad industry initially resisted jumping on the steel bandwagon so far as carbuilding was concerned, having invested large amounts of capital in woodworking shops and skilled woodworking labor. Instead, railroads accepted the use of metal in carbuilding in small doses. Some iron-framed cars began to appear in the 1880s, and as the century waned, railroads began using more metal components in their otherwise largely wooden cars. Eventually iron "truss rods" (adjustable underbody rods that strengthened wood floor sills and kept them from sagging) and center sills entered the picture. In the mid-1890s, for example, both the Baltimore & Ohio and Chicago, Burlington & Quincy began experimenting with metal sills.

Yet, right through the turn of the century and then some, carbody construction, including floors, remained largely the domain of wood. It was a sort of Catch-22

situation: more iron in a car meant greater weight and more horsepower to pull it. However, larger cars needed to be stronger to carry more freight, so more metalwork was required to increase a car's strength and durability. Gradually, carbuilders increased the use of metal, particularly steel, as it became more refined, stronger, and lighter.

The boom in the steel-making industry continued into the twentieth century, with a subsequent drop in prices for not only raw steel itself, but also the tools required to fabricate it. The change to all-steel freight-car construction accelerated when railroad accountants realized the positive economics of all-steel freight-car construction: all-steel freight cars would enable railroads to carry more tonnage with fewer cars but longer trains, fewer locomotives, fewer crew members, less maintenance costs, and longer car lives. The Golden Rule of American railroading is: If a change will save money, pursue that change.

Although there were isolated examples of all-metal freight cars dating from almost the mid-1800s, the all-steel freight car was for all practical purposes born in 1890. That year, R. P. Lamont of the Michigan Central Railroad—a component of the New York Central System—designed an all-steel boxcar while George Harvey (ironically the son of a lumber baron) actually had an all-steel gondola built by Chicago, Burlington & Quincy's shop complex at Aurora, Illinois, some 35 miles west of Chicago. Once the car had proven itself, at least to Harvey, he opened a carbuilding plant at a location on the south side of Chicago that today bears his name. His all-steel car designs were applied not only to gondolas, but also to boxcars, stockcars, and refrigerator cars. Several railroads—among them Chicago, Milwaukee & St. Paul, the Erie, the Burlington, New York Central System, and Grand Trunk Western (whose main line passes through the town of Harvey)—and a few private-car operators purchased a limited number of all-steel cars from Harvey's American Fire Proof Steel Car Company. Alas, repeat car orders never materialized to any significant degree, and the Panic of 1893 ushered in Fire Proof's untimely demise.

Harvey's endeavor was taken over by the Illinois Steel Company and reopened in 1896 as the Universal Construction Company. It began turning out all-steel

flatcars, gondolas, and hoppers. By this time, Charles Taylor and his Carnegie Steel Company was (not surprisingly) quickly becoming a proponent of all-steel railcars. Carnegie began promoting the cars to the railroad industry but met with the same indifference that had stonewalled Harvey's little company. The difference, though, was that Carnegie was no little company. Not only was it a preeminent power in the American steel industry, Carnegie had its own trunk-line railroad, the Pittsburgh, Bessemer & Lake Erie (today's Bessemer & Lake Erie).

Beginning in the late 1890s, the PB&LE became a test bed for all-steel railcars 600 of which were ordered from the Schoen Pressed Steel Company. Rated at a 50-ton capacity, the new cars were twice as expensive as wooden hoppers, but their life expectancy was twice as long. Perhaps more important, no existing hopper car was rated at 50 tons—10 tons being closer to the norm.

The PB&LE closely monitored the performance of the 600-car fleet while other railroads and carbuilders watched over its shoulder. The cars were an unqualified success, with many of them remaining in service until the end of the 1920s. PB&LE ordered more than 2,000 additional all-steel hoppers by the turn of the century. Even the omnipotent Pennsylvania Railroad was impressed and by 1906, owned some 30,000 all-steel hoppers.

Steel freight-car construction had finally caught on, and by World War I more than half of the freight cars rolling on American rails were of all-steel construction or at least had steel framing. A few stubborn nonconverts remained, with new wood-frame/body cars being produced as late as 1925. By World War II, more than 95 percent of the nation's freight-car fleet of 1.7 million cars

Freight cars formerly belonging to the Soo Line Railroad await transformation into Wisconsin Central cars at WC's shop complex near Fond du Lac, Wisconsin, in 1989. *Andover Junction Publications*

were of all-steel or steel-framed construction, although steel shortages during the war forced a return to "composite" (steel and wood) construction.

Amazingly, cars predominately of wood construction could still be found wandering the nation's railroads well into the 1960s when they were finally banished from interchange service for age reasons. In many cars, even until recent times, composite construction was employed, especially for flooring and inside wall work; nonetheless, steel had become the dominant material in freight-car construction. Early steel cars were riveted together, but as steel fabrication technologies progressed, the all-welded car became the industry standard after World War II.

The TOFC (trailer-on-flatcar) or "piggyback" train changed the face of railroading starting in the 1950s. Loaded truck trailers could be hauled over long distances by rail for less than it would cost to have truck drivers haul it the same distance, so many trucking companies began putting their trailers onto railcars. In addition, railroads' ability to haul bulk commodities cheaply remains unsurpassed, so during the post-World War II era, major power companies have increasingly turned to rail to move coal to their facilities, employing solid unit trains. In this scene on Baltimore & Ohio's main line between Cumberland, Maryland, and Cincinnati, Ohio, a coal train grinds upgrade as a *Baltimore Trailer Jet* cruises downhill with TOFCs. *Mike Schafer*

Interchange

America's early rail "network" was largely a ragtag assortment of renegade railroad companies. Few industry standards had been established, so most railroads built their own rolling stock to their specifications, reflecting their own needs. Not even George Stephenson's English "standard" track gauge of 4 feet, 8-1/2 inches was universally respected. The New York & Erie had 6-foot-gauge track while several other roads rounded off the standard gauge to 4 feet, 9 inches. In the South, trains rolled on 5-foot-gauge track.

While this worked fine for intraline (on the home road only) shipments, freight traveling across the country on more than one railroad ("interline") had to be transloaded at each railroad connecting point. The result: higher incidents of damaged "lading" (freight carried on a car) and needlessly wasted time—all at the expense of the shipper, who often had a difficult time proving the railroad was at fault. The solution to the problem was through-car operation from a shipment's point of origin to its point of destination, regardless of the number of railroads involved in moving that shipment.

For such coordination on a national scale, railroads faced a monumental undertaking. Not only would railroads have to finally agree on track gauge, but also they would have to establish at least basic standards for rolling stock: car width, height, and length; coupling devices; and braking apparatus. Further, railroads would be required to set up some sort of clerking system to keep track of not only their own cars drifting about the country, but those of other railroads whose cars were wandering on the home road's lines.

Passenger trains pioneered the through-car philosophy, since passengers were quicker to complain about train changes than was freight. As early as 1843, passengers could ride from Albany to Buffalo over seven different carriers without changing cars, and by about mid-century through freight cars were moving along the same route. The development of interline freight-car moves ("interchange") continued haphazardly until the Civil War, which forced Northern carriers into cooperating for the war effort. In some cases, this meant the relaying of track to what had become the preferred gauge of 4 feet, 8-1/2 inches. Speeding the almost overnight adaptation to wide-scale freight-car

Carbuilders

During railroading's early years, railroads built their own rolling stock, but in time, demand for freight and passenger cars began to outstrip the ability of railroads to build all that they needed. Railroads then turned to contract builders for equipment, and the commercial carbuilder was born. Some railroads continued to build their own equipment—and sometimes also buy from carbuilders—and would do so until well after World War II.

Carbuilding for railroads was a volatile business, subject to the ups and downs of the economy—and therefore the peaks and slumps in the railroads' business. During the late nineteenth century, carbuilders sprang up—and closed down—at a remarkable rate. Panics, such as those of 1873 and 1893, had devastating effects. Some companies closed for good while others simply shut down for the duration, reopening weeks or a couple of years later when business climbed back up.

As with railroads themselves, carbuilding companies were often bought out by or merged with other, sometimes larger companies. The merger between Standard Steel Car Company and the Pullman Company, for example, produced Pullman-Standard. Eventually a number of carbuilders rose to prominence, among them American Car & Foundry, Western Steel Car & Foundry, Pressed Steel Car Company, Thrall Car Manufacturing, General American Car Company, Greenville Steel Car Company, and others. Some railroads elected to stay in the carbuilding business during the steel-car era, including Santa Fe, Pennsylvania, Baltimore & Ohio, Union Pacific, Milwaukee Road, Illinois Central, Missouri-Kansas-Texas (the Katy), and Burlington, although they also relied on outside firms to bolster their car fleets.

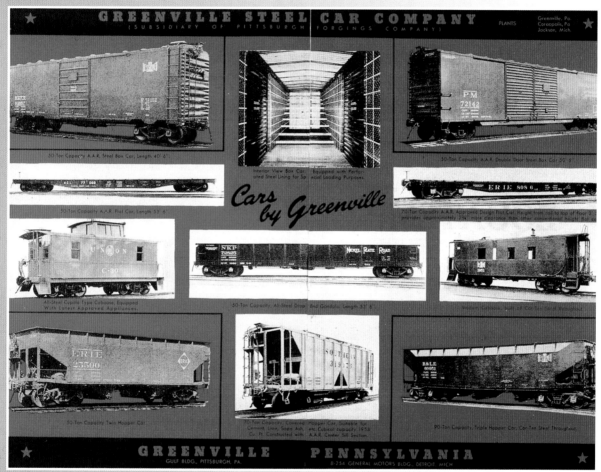

This two-page ad by Greenville Steel Car Company appeared in *Railway Age* magazine during World War II. Aside from freight cars, Greenville also built cabooses. *Mike Schafer collection*

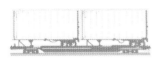

Car Types

As freight cars proliferated and new types of freight cars—or variations on existing types—were introduced, the need to keep track of cars became ever more complex, especially after interchange service became widespread in the late 1800s. Soon everybody's cars were roaming everyone else's tracks. The heyday of the freight clerk had arrived!

To reduce the amount of writing or typing required of a clerk who was monitoring freight-car movement, codes were devised to categorize and organize types of cars. So, instead of a clerk typing in that he or she was in search of a "boxcar for general service equipped with side or side and end doors" for a customer to load, the code "XM" said the same thing. This code was also used on the waybills, car-lading forms, and in freight-car register books.

Some of the basic car types and their codes are shown at right. Basically, each car category used its appropriate letter; i.e., hopper codes contained an "H", refrigerator cars an "R", and so forth. One notable exception is, of all things, the boxcar, all of which are "X" cars. Why? We can only guess that this was because there were so many boxcars, and it was simply easier and quicker to mark an "X" rather than a "B" and there was less likelihood of mistaking the "X" for any other letter. Note that auto-rack cars are considered flatcars.

Flatcars

FM	General-service flatcar
FD	Depressed-center flatcar
FC	Piggyback flat
FA	Auto-rack
LP	Bulkhead flat (pulpwood loading)

Gondolas

GB	Mill gon with either fixed or drop ends
GS	Gon with fixed sides and ends and drop bottom

Boxcars

XM	Boxcar for general service, equipped with side or side and end doors
XI	Similar to XM but insulated
XAR	Similar to XM but equipped with loading racks for loading autos and trucks
XAP	Same as XAR except equipped with racks for loading auto parts
XME	Merchandise loading, similar to XM, but wood-lined and fitted with interior appliances for stowing fixtures ("DF" equipment)
XML	Loader equipped, similar to XM, but equipped with stanchions and crossbar members for securing certain types of lading
XMP	Similar to XM, but equipped for specific commodity loading other than autos and auto parts

Refrigerator Cars

RB	Bunkerless (insulated only) refrigerator car
RBL	Similar to RB but with adjustable loading or stowing devices
RS	Bunker refrigerator cars (have ice bunkers)
RSB	Similar to RS with circulation fans and mechanical loading/unloading equipment
RSM	Similar to RS but with beef rails

Hoppers

HM	Twin hopper (two hopper bays)
HT	Triple or "quad" hopper (three or four hopper bays)
HD	Twin-dump ballast car
LO	Covered hopper

Tank Cars

TA	Tank car
TG	Tank car with glass-lined containers

Special-Service Cars

LF	Container car (well car)

interchange was the emergence of the private-car operator: nonrailroad companies that owned their own fleet of freight cars and paid the railroads to move them.

In 1867, two years after the Civil War ended, the Master Car Builders Association was created to oversee the complexities of interchange car operations. By the end of the decade, thousands of freight cars belonging to hundreds of railroads and private-car lines were freely interchanging on railroads throughout the country, with railroads making payments, based on mileage, to other railroads for moving their cars. Railroad interchange practice had been adopted on a national scale and remains in place to this day. (As an interesting side note, cars of the Pennsylvania Railroad, as owner of the largest freight-car fleet in the United States until 1968, were the most likely "foreign"-line cars to be seen on a non-PRR route.)

Standardization of Car Construction

The national interchange movement that followed the Civil War forced railroads to standardize rolling stock but only in a broad sense. A truly standardized freight car might have been achieved in a utopia, but in the real world, it was nigh impossible. There were just too many cars, and too many railroads and carbuilders building them. Instead, railroads agreed on only the degree to which they would standardize, which they would do under the guidance of the Master Carbuilders Association (MCBA). First to be standardized were the absolute necessities, such as track (and therefore wheel) gauge and coupler height. Eventually, standardization crept into such things as carbody width and height, wheel profiles, and axle and journal design. But even seemingly simple standardizations such as these resulted in ongoing confrontations among railroads, carbuilders, and the MCBA.

Some more or less internal standardization was achieved by the railroads themselves, especially larger ones that constructed their own rolling stock. Some railroads were forced into standardization when they acquired other lines, which had varying sizes of rolling stock and even track gauge. Carbuilders had more to gain from standardization and were often staunch supporters in the quest for greater standardization.

Standardization turned out to be a long, agonizing process that extended well into the twentieth century.

And like the previous century, it took a war to goad railroads to work faster at it. When the United States entered World War I in 1917, the railroads were overwhelmed by the jump in traffic. Impatient with the manner in which railroads were dealing with their new-found business, the federal government intervened, forming the United States Railroad Administration (USRA) to coordinate and outright operate most major railroads. At the same time, USRA took the best of the railroads' mechanical officers and formed a standards committee to establish design and construction standards for new locomotives and rolling stock.

The USRA scenario was viewed by many as a debacle, and USRA control ended right after the war. However, if anything good came of the USRA, some would argue that it was the establishment of equipment standards. Thousands of locomotives and cars continued to be built to USRA standards for many years after the USRA itself had vanished into the history books. By World War II, the railroads had standardized on many levels, to a degree that allowed them to operate like clockwork during the ultimate test of the American railroad: World War II. The railroads' Herculean efforts were critical to the Allied victory, and no government intervention was required.

Innovation Despite Standardization

Despite their remarkable performance during World War II, the war effort prematurely aged the railroads and left many of them in shambles. During America's postwar boom, railroads embarked on rebuilding projects as best their resources allowed. But another problem loomed large in the 1950s: the emergence of trucking (and auto) as the new transport mode of choice.

NEXT: Containers represent state-of-the-art freight transport whether by land or water. On land, by rail, containers are stacked two deep aboard well cars or spine cars. On an August day in 1996, two Union Pacific stack trains are meeting at the passing siding at Waterfall, Wyoming. A novel new concept in the 1980s, by the end of the twentieth century the stack train on many main lines had become the rule rather than the exception. *Tom Kline*

 Car Movement

Freight-car movement and utilization, like everything in railroading, is an ordered and defined system consisting of rules, standard terms, and definitions. For the clerks who keep track of roaming freight cars, the United States and Canada have been divided into 23 numbered districts. These districts consist of a state or an associated group of states and are called "home districts" for any railroad that operates in them. The clerks have to be aware of certain definitions, and for certain there are many rules to follow regarding how and which cars were to be loaded. Some basic definitions:

Home car: a car riding on the railroad to which it belongs (a Santa Fe car moving over a Santa Fe line, for example).

Foreign car: a car riding over a railroad to which it does not belong (a Santa Fe car moving on Union Pacific rails).

Private car: a car having other than railroad ownership (a UTLX—United Tank Car Line—tank car).

Per Diem the charge one railroad bills another for the use of its cars. This is computed on a daily basis. Thus if a Santa Fe car is on the Illinois Central, the Santa Fe pays the IC, say, $10 a day as long as that car is on the IC—whether loaded or empty or in transit or whatever.

Demurrage the charge a railroad assesses a shipper or consignee (receiver of goods) for holding a car too long for loading or unloading. This is also computed on a daily basis and usually begins after three days, but with Sundays and holidays free.

Some private-car owners charged railroads a flat per-mile fee instead of the per diem/demurrage agreement.

Some of the basic rules from the Association of American Railroads governing car loading and forwarding are:

Rule 1. *Do not load a car off home line if suitable foreign car of proper ownership is available or can be reasonably obtained.* (If a shipper located on the Burlington Route in Rockford, Illinois, needed a car to ship appliances to Seattle, Washington, the Burlington freight agent would attempt to locate an empty car belonging to the Great Northern, Northern Pacific, or Milwaukee Road, all three of which served Seattle.)

Rule 2. *Load foreign cars via owner roads whenever possible. Foreign cars at a junction point with owner should be loaded via owner's rails.* (Using the previous example, let's suppose the Burlington agent located an empty Great Northern boxcar; he would then route that car, once it's loaded, via the Burlington to Minneapolis where it would be turned over to the GN.)

Rule 3. *Load foreign cars to a home district.* (Again using the previous example, the Burlington agent would not have used an empty car from, say, the Pennsylvania Railroad to load for Seattle.)

Rule 4. *Load foreign cars to a district intermediate between loading point and a home district or to a district immediately adjacent to a home district.* (If a car could not be loaded to the home district proper, the agent would have loaded the car as close to one of its home districts as feasible—or at a point between where it was loaded and its home district so it could continue home once made empty.)

The above rules apply to cars in *general service*. Cars in *assigned service* must be immediately returned to their point of origin via "reverse route" (the same route they came out on) upon being made empty. That's why a car may be stenciled "Return to agent I&StLRR Peoria Ill when empty," because this car is perhaps specially equipped to handle, say, freezers from the Norge plant in Peoria to a warehouse in California.

Until this time, railroads held a virtual monopoly on freight transport in America and had been only moderately motivated to innovate. The 40-foot boxcar was king, supplemented by a court of gondolas, flatcars, tank cars, and reefers. Those railcars, in their standardized form, were good enough for moving freight before World War II, and they would be after . . . or would they? Not with the coming of age of trucking and its newly established network of federally sponsored high-speed "tracks," the Defense (Interstate) Highway System.

Suddenly, the railroads found themselves in a whole new competitive world. Now they had to truly work to win freight traffic, not only through improved service, but also with better freight cars. Existing types of freight cars had to be further improved while new types of cars (or drastically modified existing car types) had to be developed for specialized service—such as the growing intermodal business.

The railroads weren't quick to make these changes. The decline in freight traffic that followed World War II prompted railroads to focus on cost cutting rather than research and development. Not that the capital was there for R&D to begin with. The downturn in business, the outmoded work rules, and the railroad industry's unwillingness to deal with the stranglehold of federally imposed regulations dating from railroading's "robber baron" era of the late-nineteenth century had depleted resources and dulled the motivation for innovation.

Change came incrementally, first in the appearance of larger cars (as was the case early on in freight-car evolution a century earlier), and then in improved car hardware and design, such as roller-bearing trucks, mechanical (versus ice) refrigeration, and, of particular note, "cushioned underframes." Some lading is easily damaged from the shock of the car being coupled, or from "slack action" (the slack between couplers that is taken up when a train starts and returns when a train brakes) in a freight train. Something was needed to absorb and dissipate this energy. At first, springs were employed in the "draft gear" (coupler assembly and all its related rigging), but springs merely store energy momentarily and then bounce it back. Carbuilders then began adding what essentially were large shock absorbers to the draft gear; the result: the "cushioned underframe." By the early 1960s, cushioned-underframe cars—mostly boxcars, but also other car types such as auto-racks—were quickly becoming commonplace.

Eventually whole new car types emerged, such as the bi-level and tri-level auto-rack of the late 1950s, while the designs of some types of conventional car types were markedly altered for new services. Modified with special rigging to hold truck trailers, the once-lowly flatcar suddenly found itself a key component to "piggyback" or TOFC (trailer-on-flatcar) traffic—a major growth area for railroads starting in the 1950s.

With the passage of the Staggers Act in 1980, releasing the railroads from stifling government regulations, railroads were now free to pursue the traffic they really wanted and charge rates defined by the marketplace rather than the Interstate Commerce Commission. This accelerated the introduction of further-improved and even all-new freight-car types, such as the articulated "well" car so prevalent on the numerous intermodal "stack" trains that roll across American rails at the dawn of the new millennium.

The boxcar is no longer king of the rails: today it's well cars, piggyback flats, and hoppers of all types. Freight trains are fewer in number overall, and they roll on fewer lines. But the contemporary freight train is often longer—and its cars loom larger—than those of its ancestor, and today's railroads haul more tonnage than ever before in the history of American railroading.

2 Flatcars

Simple, functional, utilitarian—that's the flatcar. The most basic type of rail freight car, flatcars were the genesis for nearly all other freight-car types. Essentially a platform on wheels, flatcars could and can carry just about anything solid—lumber, stone blocks, hay bales, crates of merchandise—and for that matter liquids or powdered/ground items, too, if in barrels. Small wonder that the nation's earliest railroads relied first on flatcars to move goods.

Indeed, it appears that the first true American railroad freight car was a flatcar, on the Granite Railway of Quincy, Massachusetts. The railroad opened in 1826 and utilized stone (later, iron) rails and cars with wagon-type wheels to move slabs of granite from the quarry to the river. Initially, four-wheel flatcars were used, but as larger slabs were quarried, they were put on timber platforms that spanned two to four flatcars—in essence creating an ersatz "trucked" freight car, if you consider each four-wheel car to be a sort of de facto truck assembly. The slabs weighed nearly 65 tons apiece, and their successful transport on these 16-wheel tandem cars to the riverboats proved a railway's potential for the transport of very heavy loads—a key to the current success of railroads.

The infant Baltimore & Ohio Railroad experimented with eight-wheel flatcars in 1830. Similar to the manner in which the Granite Railway "created" an eight-wheel flatcar, B&O took two four-wheel flour cars (which, because they had low sides, technically were gondolas and not flatcars) and used them to support a specially designed platform that held cut timber. As the 1830s progressed, "baggage container cars" appeared, which were two-trucked flatcars with end railings and floor rails used to carry wood crates—tied to the floor rails—loaded with baggage. Presumably they were used on freight as well as passenger trains, although trains of the period often were one and the same.

One of the most notable American transportation endeavors of the nineteenth century was the State of Pennsylvania's Main Line of Public Works. Initially planned as an all-canal transportation artery linking Philadelphia with Pittsburgh, the ML of PW opened early in the 1830s as a combination canal/incline plane/railway system. (Incline planes were steeply inclined railways used to traverse severe mountain topography; cars were hauled up and down the incline by cable.) The flatcar would play a prominent role in the Main Line of Public Works. One of the principal drawbacks of this integrated system was that lading had to be transloaded between modes. Freight from an arriving train had to be transferred, parcel by parcel, to canal boats, and then transloaded again to incline-plane railcars, and then back to canals and so forth until the freight reached its destination. Damage to goods was rampant in any kind of transloading situation, as was theft of merchandise. The flatcar became part of the solution when John Elgar, a civil engineer from York, Pennsylvania, developed a method in which freight would be carried in a container that itself could be transloaded, thereby reducing damage to the contents. The first of these "containers" were in fact nothing more than modified boats. They were loaded with merchandise or coal or whatever, placed on a horse-drawn wagon, and then moved to the railroad where the boat was placed onto flatcars. The flatcars moved as a train to the canal, where they were routed along a special track that sloped into the canal. The flatcars were lowered into the canal by cable, and the boats simply floated off to continue their journey in the canal. Such were the primordial beginnings of intermodal transport, which would not fully catch on for more than a century.

TrailerTrain flatcars loaded with hulking farm machinery illustrate the primary virtue of the flatcar: an ability to carry large, tall, heavy loads. *Steve Smedley*

"Fishbelly" side sills of steel-framed flatcars such as Pennsylvania car No. 470318 provided added strength much like truss rods did on wood-frame cars. In this scene from 1931, the flatcar is being used to haul containers, proving that the containerization concept isn't as new as one might expect. *Pennsylvania Railroad, Mike Del Vecchio collection*

By the 1850s, a pair of four-wheel swivel trucks were the norm on freight cars. Flatcars had iron side sills by this time, and early photos show cast-iron stake pockets along the side sills, which allowed the temporary placement of stakes so as to keep the freight—especially loose items like lumber—from sliding off the car. The stake pockets could also be used to tie down loads with rope. Car length in this period was about 25 feet, with widths close to 8 feet.

The popularity of the flatcar as the jack-of-all-trades freight car was short-lived once the gondola and boxcar had evolved from it. Thereafter, flatcars were used main-ly to carry items unaffected by weather and temperature, especially items of great weight, height, width, or length. Boxcar capacity was limited by the car sides and roofs, but just about anything could be piled high on a flatcar. To a limited degree, the width of the freight being carried could breach the width of the car, while height was limited in part by tunnel and overhead bridge clearances. In the case of extralong items (such as rail or pipe), two or more adjacent flatcars could carry the load.

Such flexibility of service rendered short lives to flatcars. In the early years of railroading, the load limit of a flatcar was often violated, sometimes with dire

Piggybacking is another "new" concept that actually dates to the early twentieth century. Chicago North Shore & Milwaukee, a Midwestern electric interurban line operating between Chicago and Milwaukee until 1963, is often cited as one of the pioneers of piggybacking, as this scene from circa 1930 suggests. *Greg Heier collection*

results—overloaded cars could collapse, especially in a sudden start or stop that produced severe slack action between coupled cars. Flatcars probably were among the earliest car types to employ truss rods to strengthen the car's middle. On the plus side, flatcars were certainly the cheapest of car types to build.

Flatcar evolution was modest at best. The standard flatcar for the bulk of the twentieth century was either 40 or 50 feet long and close to 10 feet wide. Even in the steel-car era, flatcars almost always featured wood plank flooring and had provisions for stakes and tie-downs.

Over the decades, flatcars pretty much remained the straightforward platforms on wheels that folks still associate with their name, but the post–World War II era ushered in some changes that put them in a new light. The most notable was the use of the flatcar to haul truck trailers in intermodal service. Not that the trailer-on-flatcar (TOFC) concept was a postwar invention—railroads had experimented with the transport of truck trailers as early as the mid-1920s if not before. But not until after the war did TOFC traffic catch on in a big way, largely due to a venture known as "TrucTrain,"

Santa Fe flatcar No. 330269, photographed at Montgomery, Texas, in May 1988, illustrates a typical 40-foot bulkhead flatcar, here loaded with pulpwood. The high ends help secure the lading and keep it from shifting. Other commodities commonly found on bulkhead flats included dimensional lumber, wallboard, and plywood. *Tom Kline*

It's February 1966—the early years of railroading's soon-to-boom piggyback era—as Chicago & North Western train No. 381 trundles through Nelson, Illinois, en route from Chicago to St. Louis with a then-typical 85-foot TrailerTrain flatcar loaded with two classic C&NW truck trailers. North Western was an early promoter of piggyback service using its own trailers. *Mike McBride*

introduced in 1954 by the Pennsylvania Railroad (PRR)—which, by the way, owned more flatcars than any of its contemporaries.

PRR's TrucTrains were all-piggyback runs that carried both PRR-owned truck trailers as well as those of common-carrier truck lines. The trains were run on strict, express-type schedules similar to a passenger train. The low tariffs allowed trucking companies to move their trailers over long distances cheaper than if they paid a driver to do so over the highway.

Although truck trailers often were hauled on conventional flatcars, specially equipped flatcars were developed exclusively for TOFC service. As such,

RIGHT: GBRX 9038 at Tecific, Texas, in 1991 shows the evolution of the basic bulkhead flatcar design with the addition of a center beam or "spine." This center divider added strength, allowing for a longer car and larger loads, and helped stabilize the lading. Such cars were used almost universally for bundled lumber. *Gerald Hook*

LEFT: Demonstrating the flatcar's chief claim to fame—its ability to carry extremely large, heavy, tall loads such as the transformer riding this Penn Central car—is the depressed-center flat. Photographed at Katy, Texas, in October 1979, this car is equipped with Buckeye-style trucks featuring six-wheel hinged trucks built to handle extremely heavy loads. The extra set of wheels helped spread out the weight while the hinging arrangement allowed the three axles to move independent of one another on rough track or a switch. *Gerald Hook*

TOFC flats had channeled floors to guide the wheels of trailers being rolled into position; they also featured a "fifth wheel" to support the forward end of the trailer as well as other tie-down appliances to keep trailers from bouncing off the flats. The standard flatcar length of 40-50 feet was stretched to 85 feet to accommodate two trailers. Early TOFC flats also featured flop-down wheel aprons at each end that allowed trailers to be driven the length of a string of coupled flats for ease of loading. Today, cranes are used to lift trailers on and off the flats. Interestingly, single-trailer flatcars have signaled the return of a car format that had vanished in the nineteenth century: four-wheel cars.

Overshadowed by the boxcars early on, flatcars today have made a big comeback, thanks to the boom in intermodal traffic. In today's modern freight trains, you are probably more likely to spot a flatcar than a boxcar.

What happens when a load exceeds the length of even the longest flatcar? That was the challenge facing Standard Oil Company, the consignee of this huge oil tank being shipped from a point on the Lehigh Valley Railroad to the Standard Oil facility on the Pennsylvania Railroad at Whiting, Indiana, in the late 1940s. Three flatcars were employed, two 50-foot cars sandwiching a 30-foot "idler" flat used primarily to space the two load-bearing flats. The two 70-ton, 50-foot flats in this scene were particularly durable cars, since their entire carbodies (except for the wood decking) were cast in one piece from huge sand molds. *Lehigh Valley Railroad, Mike Del Vecchio collection*

3 Gondolas

Like its cousin, the flatcar, the gondola is among the most utilitarian of freight-car types. In its most basic form, the gondola is merely a flatcar with sides—but what a difference sides can make! Now just about anything could be loaded into the car without concern for it sliding off. The gondola could hold objects such as crates of freight, or it could handle loose, bulk material like gravel or coal.

Dating from about 1830, gondolas were first used on early railways and tramways to move coal. In hauling loose mineral matter, early gons were somewhat limited because there was no easy way to unload the cars, hence the development of the hopper car, which is in essence a modified gondola.

Photos from the mid-1800s show that early gondolas often were nothing more than a flatcar to which low (perhaps about two feet) wooden sides had been added atop the flatcar floor. By about the Civil War, drop-bottom gondolas appeared, making it easier to unload aggregate, coal, ore, or other similar bulk material. Instead of men having to shovel the contents out over the sides, floor hatches allowed the material to escape—though manpower was still required to shovel the contents toward the hatches.

Like most other freight cars, the size and capacity of the gondola increased over the years. Until the post–Civil War period, gons tended to be less than 30 feet long with a capacity of about 15 tons. By the end of the century,

Gondolas are prominent in this scene at Milwaukee Road's shop complex in the railroad's namesake city circa 1940. The crane is loading ash and cinders from the ash pits into waiting gons, while the gondolas farther back are loaded with coal that will be transferred to the adjacent coal chute. Gondolas were near the bottom of the freight-car "seniority list" in terms of hauling freight of high esteem. They were (and are) best suited for dense, heavy bulk material and scrap metal. *Milwaukee Road, Mike Del Vecchio collection*

A classic 40-foot steel gon, Pittsburgh & West Virginia car No. 7770 at Toledo, Ohio, in January 1962 typifies gondola construction from about World War I to the late twentieth century. The car has eleven panels on each side, separated by ribs that provide extra strength. Gons like this were used to carry everything from finished mill products to scrap iron. In the early part of the century, these cars commonly carried coal and usually were unloaded with a clamshell crane. *Hank Goerke*

Covered gondolas are used to move moisture-sensitive lading. Milwaukee Road 360751 is a 50-foot covered gon with a 70-ton capacity converted from an older car. This car was originally built in February 1930 as an open-top composite gondola very much like those in the photo that opens this chapter. In the conversion, the wooden sides were removed and plate steel welded to the existing steel braces. A cover with hatches and a roofwalk (for brakemen) was fabricated and welded in place. This particular type of conversion was unique to the Milwaukee Road. The car is shown in 1953, probably at the railroad's famous Milwaukee Shops following its makeover. *Milwaukee Road Historical Association*

Missouri-Kansas-Texas No. 16602 at Belle Meade, Texas, in 1988 is a 14-panel gondola with fishbelly side sills. The engineering design on this car was similar to the trusses of a steel bridge and kept the car from sagging from abuses during loading. Cars like this commonly had wood floors, which did not have the corrosion problems of steel and were easily replaced when damaged. Gons were particularly prone to abuse since they were used to carry heavy, bulky freight. Note how the sides of this car have bulged out due to rough loading. *Tom Kline*

gons were approaching the 36-foot mark with a capacity of 25-30 tons. For much of the steel-car era during the first half of the twentieth century, 40- and 50-foot gons were the norm with a capacity of about 50-70 tons. The side height of gondolas usually reflected the purpose for which they were intended. Two-foot-high sides prevented cars from being overloaded with heavy sand or gravel. Cars used to haul pipe had 6-foot sides and end bulkheads.

Construction evolved so that the gon was no longer a flatcar with sides. Steel gons were built in the same manner as truss bridges, in which a steel center sill and cross-members supported steel-plate car sides. The side sills—often "fishbellied" for added strength—bore much of the weight of the lading along with the sides themselves. Wood planking, however, continued to be popular for flooring. Wood was more corrosion-resistant than steel flooring, could better absorb the shocks of rough loading, and was easily replaced.

During World War II, the composite (steel-framed/wood-side) gondola reappeared as a "war emergency"

Among the interesting vintage freight cars in this westbound Northern Pacific train out of Livingston, Montana, in 1941 are two 40-foot, 50-ton NP drop-bottom gons loaded with coal. The fingerlike devices lining the bottom sides of each car are latches for opening the hatches. Note the ancient round-roof wood boxcar, complete with underbody truss rods, just ahead of the gons. *Northern Pacific, Mike Del Vecchio collection*

car. Plate steel was in high demand, so carbuilders reverted to the composite construction techniques that had immediately preceded the all-steel car era. Many composite gons remained in service well into the second half of the twentieth century.

As with other car types, the standard gondola format often was modified by carbuilders for special applications. Drop ends allowed for extra long loads (other drop-end gons or flat cars had to be coupled adjacent to accommodate the overhang). While regular open-top gons were fine for handling such dense, heavy cargo as scrap metal, crated freight, ceramic piping, brick, cable reels, and rail, covered gons were used to carry similar heavy items that

required protection from direct moisture. Newly rolled steel that was to be used in food-product containers or similar applications where it had to be absolutely rust free was an ideal candidate for the covered gondola.

Often mistaken for hoppers and sometimes looking like doorless boxcars (which in fact some are; see photos), high-sided gondolas were used to transport lightweight bulk commodities such as wood chips. Today, coal is commonly hauled in high-sided gondolas that look like hopper cars. However, without hatched hopper bottoms, these are technically gondolas, which are unloaded by special equipment that literally rotates the car upside down to instantly empty it.

Sturdy Boston & Maine 9071 is a 52-foot gon with a 100-ton capacity, photographed at Marion, Ohio, only two months after it was constructed—note there are few dings or dents. The car features a heavy top chord (the lip around the top of the car) with tie-down loops, and hefty ribs—all necessary for strength. B&M's famous Minuteman herald provides a nice touch to this colorful car. *David P. Oroszi*

This Detroit, Toledo & Ironton gon is a 50-footer with a 70-ton capacity. Built in 1951, it has been converted to haul coil steel, as evidenced by the removable coil covers, necessary to protect the steel from moisture. Steel used in the production of tin cans, for example, had to be protected from rusting. *Hank Goerke*

OPPOSITE TOP: At a glance from ground level, this sky-blue car belonging to Gas Management Properties at Gloster, Mississippi, in 1987 might appear to be a boxcar with a lot of wood chips on the roof—but the lack of doors confirms this to be a wood-chip gondola. In fact, this car was once indeed a boxcar and was later converted for wood-chip service (look closely and you can see where newer steel panelwork covers what had been the door openings). Note, too, that the trucks have been converted to roller bearing, but were using the original friction-bearing sideframes. *Gerald A. Hook*

What appears to be a hopper car in a modern-day coal train that has arrived at Houston Lighting & Power Company (background) on a March day in 1993 is technically a high-sided gondola, as the car has no bottom hopper wells and hatches. Unloading is accomplished through a special unloading device that rotates the car in place without being uncoupled from adjacent cars. This requires a special rotating coupler at one end of the car, and all such couplers must be at the same end in a train. The red paint denotes the ends that have the rotating couplers, so it is easy for crews to see a car that was not properly pointed. *Tom Kline*

4 Boxcars and Stockcars

Second only to the now-vanished caboose, the boxcar is an icon of American freight railroading. For the better part of 150 years, the boxcar reigned as an integral part of everyday railroading. Only during the last two decades of the twentieth century has the boxcar's importance taken a back seat in the transport of the nation's freight, thanks to the rise of the intermodal truck trailer and container as the preferred conveyance.

Unlike the flatcar and the gondola, both of which can trace their origins to England, the boxcar appears to be largely an American phenomenon. Initially, flatcars and gondolas dominated the railroad scene, but America's harsh weather conditions, coupled with the high incidence of cargo fires resulting from wood-burning locomotives, spurred the development of the enclosed freight car. England's relatively mild year-round climate and the widespread use of coke-burning locomotives precluded such a development.

Early enclosed cars were but high-sided gondolas with canvas covers, but early in the 1830s, a few of America's pioneering railroads explored the viability of "house" cars, which with their high-pitched roofs resembled rolling abodes. One of these trailblazing companies was the Mohawk & Hudson, the genesis railroad of the future New York Central System. Around 1833, the M&H introduced the covered gondola, a stubby (12 feet long), doorless, four-wheel, round-roof vehicle that resembled a gypsy wagon; freight was loaded through a removable car end. The railroad built a fleet of these

In 1963, when this scene was recorded on the New York Central Railroad near Detroit, Michigan, boxcars were still the most prominent freight car in the land. In many cases, bright colors like those of the cars at left had replaced the drab reds and browns of an earlier era, represented by boxcars trailing the two Electro-Motive diesels. The new "hot" color in early 1960s railroading was Jade Green, worn by the two NYC boxcars at left. *Hank Goerke*

46

Three wood boxcars photographed around the turn of the century illustrate the varied appearances of pre-steel-era rolling stock. True standardization was still several years away, but the cars still share some common ground. All three ride on archbar trucks, and all three sport truss rods (visible under the car floor), a common means of strengthening a car's underframe. The 34-foot Cincinnati, Hamilton & Dayton car at far left is marked for grain service. The New Orleans & North Eastern car (center) is also a 34-foot car. The Kansas City, Mexico & Orient car illustrates early "high-cube" (high cubic-foot capacity) for bulky loads and appears to be about 37 feet long. *David P. Oroszi Collection*

Probably among the last fleets of intact 1930s-era outside-braced wood-side boxcars were those belonging to shortline Wellsville, Addison & Galeton. Purchased secondhand from the Boston & Maine, the cars were still in interchange service in the 1970s. The railroad served several tanneries in Pennsylvania, and so carried WAG's famous slogan, "The Sole Leather Line." WAG 5017 is spotted for unloading at the Cutsole, a shoe factory along the Chicago & North Western in Dixon, Illinois, in 1974. *Mike McBride*

Two boxcars of the New York, Susquehanna & Western at Jersey City, New Jersey, circa World War II show the difference between a single-sheathed (outside-braced) composite boxcar from earlier in the century and a new all-steel boxcar. On the former, the steel underbody framework provided most of the car's (and lading's) support, while in the newer car, the sheet-panel steel sides and dreadnaught end panels helped provide support. *Railroad Avenue Enterprises, Mike Del Vecchio collection*

cars, which some consider to be the predecessor of the modern boxcar. M&H had a special need for cars that protected freight from snow: the railroad did most of its hauling during winter months when the paralleling Erie Canal was frozen over.

By the end of the 1830s, the enclosed freight car was catching on with a number of carriers, even in the sunny South. By this time, the boxcar had evolved to having a considerably larger carbody—with side doors—riding on two four-wheel trucks. Baltimore & Ohio's famous Mount Clare (Maryland) shops are often credited with refining boxcar designs of that period. Boxcars generally were less than 30 feet long and 7 feet wide and with no more than a 10-ton capacity. By the time of the Civil War, the popularity of boxcars had been well established.

As noted in chapter 1, the Civil War mobilized the nation's railroads, forcing them to operate as a more-unified

Text continued on page 54

Introduced after World War II, the PS-1 boxcar was based on a 1939 design and for over 30 years would be the most common boxcar type to roam the rails. Workers at the Pullman-Standard plant near Chicago put the finishing touches on the first P-S-built PS-1 car in 1947. *Pullman-Standard, Mike Del Vecchio collection*

Many roads used their boxcars as rolling billboards for their passenger trains. Chicago & North Western 701 is advertising the road's *"400"* fleet of streamliners as it rolls eastward through Dixon, Illinois, in 1975. *Mike McBride*

In the early 1930s, the Pennsylvania Railroad wanted to build cars with increased inside heights, but ran into line-clearance problems. The solution was to round off the corners of the roof along the sides. PRR built over 10,000 of these "round roof" cars in various configurations. The Detroit, Toledo & Ironton and Norfolk & Western railroads also received round-roof cars since those two roads were controlled by the PRR at the time. Most of the roundtops were retired early in the 1960s, but some were converted to stockcars and lasted a little longer. Some of the DT&I cars were subsequently sold to other railroads, such as Northern Pacific. *Mike Del Vecchio collection*

Northern Pacific No. 28842 is a war-emergency boxcar, built using wood and steel components to conserve steel. It still looks good in August 1965. NP's fleet survived about the longest, lasting into the late 1960s. *Roy Klaus, David P. Oroszi collection*

 ## Boxcars as
Railroad Billboards

Several railroads applied their diesel-locomotive and/or passenger-train colors to their boxcars. Great Northern will long be remembered for its handsome Pullman Green and Omaha Orange colors, which first showed up on World War II-era diesels and then in 1947 on its first streamliner, the *Empire Builder*. The colors later appeared on some boxcars, as illustrated in this 1961 photo. *Hank Goerke*

Throughout most of the first century of American railroading, freight-car livery has pretty much bordered on "mundane." For decades, railroads stuck to using solid, somber colors to paint their freight rolling stock—usually dull oxide reds, browns, and blacks. Although the technology was there for brighter colors, they were more costly and their pigmentation less stable. Besides, railroads had *lots* of freight cars to paint, so cost-effective paints were the first choice of many railroads. The brilliant exceptions were operators of privately owned car fleets, such as those of refrigerator-car companies and breweries.

Eventually railroads came to realize that their freight-car fleet—especially boxcars with their large, flat sides—could serve as free advertising for the railroad. Bolder lettering and slogans began to appear, giving folks stopped by passing trains something to read about. "Route of the Chief" proclaimed Santa Fe boxcars, hoping to entice the family waiting for the train to go by to choose the *Chief* on their next vacation to California. "Frisco Fast Freight" might inspire shippers to route their next load of washing machines via the St. Louis-San Francisco Railway.

After World War II, many railroads opted for brighter colors and more complex schemes for selected members of their freight-car fleet. New York Central, for example, introduced its memorable red-and-gray "Pacemaker" boxcars touting its new high-speed merchandise service. Great Northern was one of several roads in the 1960s to embrace Jade Green, the hot new color in modern railroading.

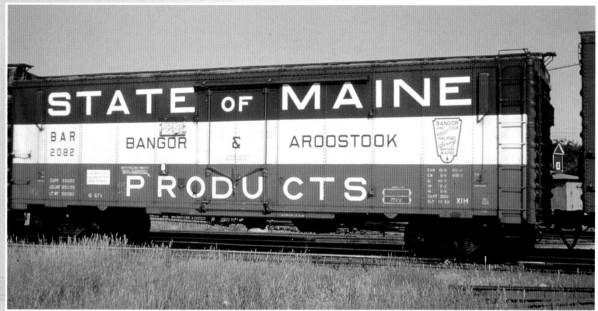

One of the most famous colorful freight-car schemes was that of the red, white, and blue "State of Maine" Bangor & Aroostook boxcars, dating from the late steam era. The New Haven Railroad also owned State of Maine-scheme boxcars, by virtue of tacking its car order onto that of the Bangor & Aroostook. Apparently because of setup costs, the carbuilder told NH that it would be cheaper to go with the red, white, and blue livery than the standard boxcar brown that NH had requested, and NH went patriotic. *Hank Goerke*

Great Northern had one of the most colorful boxcar fleets, with cars in several different paint schemes over the years. One of these was the vermilion scheme shown here in April 1961 on GN 13475. When new, the cars were stunning with their billboard lettering and mountain-goat emblem. Not quite as colorful, but just as interesting, is the rocket-scheme Toledo, Peoria & Western 608 coupled to it. These cars featured two slogans, "Links East and West" and "The Transcontinental Peoria Way." Only a few TP&W boxcars were painted like this. *Hank Goerke*

Northern Pacific 97576 is a 50-foot plug-door (a door that seals when shut) boxcar. Built in 1964, it proclaims NP's fame as the "Scenic Route of the North Coast Limited." *Roy Klaus, David P. Oroszi collection*

Text continued from page 49

system. The real turning point came around 1870 with the establishment of formal interchange service and agreements. Freight cars traveled farther as interline movements became widespread, and there arose a greater need for durability, standardization, and—with the ongoing boom in traffic—greater capacity, both in terms of weight and dimension. Fortunately, these needs coincided with the refinement of metalworking and steel making as well as improved car construction techniques. So, by the end of the nineteenth century, the boxcar's load capacity had more than quadrupled to 40-50 tons—even though the weight of the car itself ("light weight") might have only increased a fraction of that.

An early boxcar variation was the high-cubic-foot-capacity car, which first appeared during the Civil War era when B&O built a larger-than-normal boxcar to carry empty barrels. Higher and sometimes longer than a traditional boxcar and featuring larger doors, "high-cube" boxcars were ideal for lightweight but space-consuming commodities such as furniture.

By the end of the nineteenth century, legions of boxcars moved the nation's freight. In 1900 for example, the B&O owned some 60,000 freight-carrying cars, nearly half of which were boxcars. Railroads loved boxcars and at that time owned more of them than any other car type. Just about anything could be carried in a boxcar, including liquids (if in barrels) and grain—loose—thanks to special grain-door attachments that kept the grain from flowing out through the doors.

Standardization

The evolution of turn-of-the-century 36-foot boxcars into the standard 40-foot steel car, which was the hallmark of railroading well into the second half of the twentieth century, is the result of several indirectly related improvements. One was the Bessemer steel-making process, which made steel available cheaply and—together with the adoption of the automatic (knuckle) coupler and air brake in the late

One-year-plus-old Wabash 55054 moving eastbound on a Norfolk & Western freight at Hammond, Indiana, represented the state-of-the-art high-cubic-foot boxcar in 1965. The 89-foot (93 feet including couplers) "Hi-Cubes," as they were marketed, had an inside length of over 86 feet. They were intended for auto-parts service and were found on railroads that served major auto assembly plants; 28 railroads were involved in the design of the Hi-Cube. This Wabash car and its sisters cost $35,000 each and were almost certainly among the last rolling stock ever ordered by the railroad, which had been merged into Norfolk & Western in the fall of 1964. *Mike McBride*

nineteenth century—allowed for cars of greater capacity and longer trains.

Early in the twentieth century, many American railroads designed their own cars for their own needs— a primary reason why cars of that era looked so different. The first widespread standardization resulted from the United States Railroad Administration, which operated the nation's railroads during World War I. USRA also established locomotive and rolling-stock standards to reduce costs, enabling carbuilders to build quickly and efficiently and yet create cars of high quality. USRA boxcars were composite cars of varying designs with heavy underframes.

In the early 1920s, the Pennsylvania and New York Central railroads offered designs for standardized 40-foot steel boxcars to the American Railway Association (later the Association of American Railroads), but the railroads could not agree on a final design, and each continued building cars of their own designs. Not until 1932 did the ARA come up with a new design for a 40-foot all-steel boxcar that was widely accepted as standard by most American railroads. The car was very successful and became, with its myriad modifications over the years, the most popular boxcar ever produced. Pullman-Standard's version of this car, based on a 1939 AAR updated design, was known as the PS-1, production of which began in the late 1940s once World War II steel restrictions were lifted.

The PS-1 was significant for several reasons. First, it was two tons lighter than similar previous cars. The car's framing was lighter because the car's steel "skin" was, in part, load bearing. Corrugated "dreadnaught" car ends

Several railroads built their own freight cars well after most other roads began buying from any of the several large carbuilders that had been established during the early part of the twentieth century. One of these do-it-yourselfers was the Milwaukee Road, which built much of its own rolling stock, from passenger cars to freight cars to cabooses. A hallmark of Milwaukee Road-built equipment was rib sides, plainly visible in this circa-1940 scene at the railroad's famous Milwaukee Shops. The ribbing was more than decorative: it made possible lighter vertical bracing that saved thousands of pounds. *Mike Keim, Mike Del Vecchio collection*

Looking a bit faded in this 1986 photo, Atchison, Topeka & Santa Fe 190019 is a rebuild of a United States Railroad Administration double-sheathed boxcar (two walls sandwiching a framework, rather than self-supporting single sides of later cars). These rebuilds were carried out at the road's Topeka (Kansas) Shops in the late 1930s and early 1940s. Many roads rebuilt their URSA cars, but Santa Fe did the most with over 2,600 conversions. *Steve Smedley*

Rather than retire all of its 1920s-era boxcars after World War II, Missouri Pacific rebuilt a number of them for its "Eagle Merchandise Service," a less-than-carload (LCL) operation that offered tightly scheduled service for shippers on Mopac lines. Revamped cars such as MP 12069 shown circa 1950 (possibly at St. Louis) received the railroad's blue-and-gray passenger scheme and special livery and were operated on specific MP routes on scheduled freights. *MP, Mike Del Vecchio collection*

added further strength, and the center sill was also lighter since it did not bear the entire weight of the lading.

Because this car was an agreed-upon standard design, any carbuilder could construct from these plans, thereby reducing costs. Also, the PS-1 employed fully standardized appliances (doors, roofs, brake rigging, couplers, etc.), and all-steel cars in general required far less maintenance than their wooden predecessors, resulting in more cost savings. Thus, the railroads were able to buy boxcars of proven and accepted design off the shelf cheaper than custom designing and building their own. These innovations changed the railroad freight-car scene forever.

Although 40-foot boxcars could be found roaming the rails until the end of the twentieth century, variations on the standard 40-foot theme emerged early in the century. One of the earliest was the double door, which greatly facilitated the loading or unloading of large or unwieldy freight—for example, a bundle of 18-foot 2 x 6s. Nearly all boxcars assigned to furniture, automobile, and lumber service were thus equipped with double doors. Post-1950 boxcars usually featured 8- or 10-foot doors so that lift trucks could unload them, and the introduction of plug doors allowed boxcars to be completely sealed from outside dust and dirt. Some boxcars featured end doors in addition to their

Money-making advantages to
RAILROADS and SHIPPERS

DF-B EQUIPMENT IS EASY
TO OPERATE

One man can unlock, position and lock bulkheads in place. Lading can be loaded quicker and easier . . . shippers save on labor costs.

DF-B EQUIPMENT PERMITS
FASTER LOADING

One-lever operation simultaneously locks and unlocks all four pins in bulkhead. Bulkheads can be positioned and locked in just a few moves. They can be placed flat against walls of car or doorway area for maximum room . . . fork-lift trucks can load and unload more efficiently.

DF-B EQUIPPED CARS ARE
EASY TO MAINTAIN

The few working parts of Evans DF-B bulkheads are accessible for easy and fast maintenance.

DF-B EQUIPMENT IS VERSATILE

Evans DF-B equipment can be installed in common, insulated or refrigerator cars—new or existing cars. And nearly all packaged or palletized commodities can be safely carried—damage-free!

DF-B EQUIPMENT VIRTUALLY
ELIMINATES DAMAGE

DF-B equipped cars handle lading with the famous "Kid Glove Treatment."® Shipping damage is virtually eliminated . . . railroads save money on damage claims, the replacement of damaged consignments by shippers is cut to a minimum, and shippers get further business from satisfied customers. Damaged shipments can cause customers to go elsewhere. DF-B equipped cars ensure the safe arrival of your goods!

DF-B EQUIPMENT COSTS SHIPPERS
NOTHING EXTRA

Both railroad and shippers like DF-B equipment. There's no extra charge, because railroads have discovered that damage-free cars create more business, bring in more revenue per year than common cars. And shippers can load cars to capacity—safely!

This Union Pacific double-door boxcar has had its roof raised to increase inside height. Many railroads modified their existing car fleets as necessary to accommodate the changing needs of their shippers. This was done in situations involving only a small number of cars when buying a new design would not justify the costs. UP 517050 is at the rear of a southbound Illinois Central freight at Dixon, Illinois, in 1968. *Mike McBride*

side doors, allowing things like tractors and autos to be easily driven into the boxcar.

To reduce damage owing to cargo being jostled around during a journey, carbuilders began to equip some boxcars with special interior fixtures, such as tiedowns, that allowed the freight to be secured. Other, more elaborate systems incorporated adjustable shelving arrangements within the car or moveable bulkheads, all designed to keep the freight from shifting during sudden starts and stops—a major cause of damaged lading.

Insulated boxcars came into wide use after World War II for the transport of items requiring moderate, consistent temperatures. Bottled beer and canned

This page from an Evans Product Company brochure illustrates the moveable bulkhead arrangement found in modern boxcars. The bulkheads, which could be adjusted and moved about by one person, greatly reduced shifted loads and damage. *Tom Kline collection*

goods, for example, don't require refrigeration per se during shipment, but they do need to be protected from subfreezing or excessively hot outside temperatures. Previously, such items had been moved in noniced refrigerator cars, but since this disrupted the reefer supply, the insulated boxcar emerged, utilizing new technologies of insulation.

The 50-foot boxcar began to catch on in the late 1930s, especially for the movement of lumber, and by the 1980s, the 50-footer had become almost as familiar as the 40-foot boxcar. Boxcar size had reached its zenith, though, early in the 1960s, with the introduction of the 89-foot "Hi-Cube" boxcar, which took the high-cubic-foot format to new heights. Developed with auto manufacturers in mind, these behemoths can accommodate large volumes of space-consuming but relatively light-weight auto parts such as fender stampings.

One of the most visible postwar design changes in the ubiquitous boxcar was outside-braced construction

featuring a supporting framework—vertical steel members—welded to the outsides of the car walls. This allowed for even stronger, more durable boxcars with greater weight capacity.

Stockcars

Used for moving livestock—especially cattle and pigs—the stockcar was in essence a well-ventilated boxcar. The movement of livestock by rail dates from the 1830s, but the development of cars designed specifically for livestock transport came several decades later. Meanwhile, cattle were moved in either high-sided gondolas or boxcars equipped with slatted doors for ventilation—cars intended for the transport of produce, not cattle. Prior to the Civil War, combination cattle/boxcars appeared, some of which were used for (perish the thought) hauling grain when not being used for cattle transport.

Early in the 1860s, the "pure" stockcar took hold, following a format that would remain for the next century: a roofed car with fully slatted (usually horizontal) sides and doors. Some cars featured removable upper-level floors, thereby creating a double-deck car. With the special floors in place, the car could haul two levels of "short" livestock such as sheep or pigs. With the upper floor removed, the car would be made suitable for horses and cows. Aside from ventilation, the slatted sides allowed the livestock to be hosed down at servicing stops, a necessary treatment in hot weather.

From the 1870s to the turn of the century, stockcars grew in similar manner to their boxcar cousin. Post–Civil War stockcars generally were less than 30

61

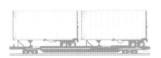

Incentive Per-diem Boxcars

To address a nationwide shortage of clean, usable boxcars in the 1970s, the Interstate Commerce Commission introduced an additional per-diem compensation factor in the amount a host railroad paid the owner of a car for every day the car was on the host road's line. Furthermore, once made empty, the car did not have to return to the home railroad. It could be used for another shipment regardless of the direction of travel.

It was hoped that these new incentives would prompt railroads everywhere to buy new boxcars to use for additional income. However, the plan drew little response from the big Class I carriers while shortline railroads—though quite interested in the plan—lacked the necessary funding to build or purchase new cars themselves.

Venture capital groups did take notice, but since the arrangement applied only to cars belonging to railroads, they had to find a loophole to take advantage of the generous new per-diem revenue. They did this by purchasing new cars and leasing them to shortlines for about $300-$400 per month—an amount that shortlines were more than happy to pay, since each car earned upwards of $20 a day, or about $600 per month. A fleet of 100 cars thus could net the shortline up to about $30,000 a month—a tidy sum for little railroads struggling to make ends meet.

Many shortlines jumped at the opportunity, and by the late 1970s one could see colorful boxcars from a multitude

Though only some 40 miles long, Ashley, Drew & Northern was one of numerous shortlines that took advantage of the per-diem incentive rates established in the 1970s. Boxcars such as this at Crosset, Arkansas, in 1979 belonging to the Arkansas-based carrier were for years a common sight throughout the United States. *Gerald Hook*

of otherwise obscure carriers out on foreign rails making money for their owner(s). Many of these cars might not visit home rails for months at a time—which was good news on more than one front. Once on home rails, the cars were no longer making the special per-diem incentive rate; further, some shortlines owned more cars than could fit on all their track—a massive logistical problem should all of its cars happen to migrate home at the same time!

feet long and could carry 20,000 pounds of livestock. By the end of the century, stockcars were approaching 40 feet and could carry 30 tons of doomed animals.

That was a lot of hooves kicking around in a single car, and during the late 1800s a public cry arose for more humane treatment of livestock being moved by rail—despite the irony of their journey. The result was the "Palace" car (a takeoff on the luxury "palace cars"

being built for passenger trains by Pullman), which featured water and feed troughs. Other "humane" cars featured pens to isolate the animals from one another, since trampling was a major cause of injury.

During the twentieth century, stockcar design did not change very much, save for the introduction of steel-framed and later all-steel cars. Wood remained popular for the slatted sides, although flat steel bars

A trio of stockcars rides the forward end of an east-bound Milwaukee Road freight meeting the *City of Los Angeles* near Davis Junction, Illinois, in August 1958. Stockcars riding in a train of mixed freight were often positioned immediately behind the locomotives so that they could easily be switched out of the train when it was time to water, feed, and rest the stock. It also made for a less-jolting ride. *Howard Patrick*

Stockcars have become extremely rare as the twentieth century closes, but a fine example of a classic stockcar from earlier in the century exists in the tiny burgh of Bud Matthews, Texas. As the double doors reveal, this is a double-deck car once used for hauling sheep or pigs. The former Santa Fe car stands on an isolated piece of former Texas Central (later, Missouri-Kansas-Texas) track at a cattle-loading facility. The railroad pulled out in 1967, but cattle are still loaded at Bud Matthews, onto trucks. *Gerald A. Hook*

were also used. Some cars featured sheet steel sides, as in a regular boxcar, but stamped with ventilation slots.

With the decentralization of the meatpacking industry and the subsequent growth in the frozen food industry, the movement of livestock by rail plummeted after World War II. As trips between livestock ranches and meat-processing plants shortened, the railroads became even more vulnerable to trucking in the live-stock trade. The railroads were increasingly anxious to get rid of livestock traffic by this time anyway, since the manpower and acreage required for livestock handling were costly. On long trips, cattle had to be unloaded at wayside pens periodically for rest, water, and feeding as mandated by federal laws. By the 1980s, livestock movement by rail had become rare, and by the end of the twentieth century had become virtually nonexistent, along with the stockcar.

5 Reefers

Although the refrigerator car, or "reefer," is another close cousin of the boxcar, it is among the most interesting of freight cars and deserves its own chapter. The impact that the refrigerator car had on the American diet is probably vastly underestimated.

When it became clear in the mid-nineteenth century that the railroad was destined to be *the* eminent form of transportation for anything imaginable—from people to cows to merchandise—railroads and shippers began devising ways of moving food products. This was not nearly as easy as figuring out ways to move, for example, kegs of nails (put them in a gondola), a dozen roll-top desks (stuff them in a boxcar), or 10 tons of coal (dump it in a hopper). For all its good points, food has a nasty habit of decaying, whether it's fresh-cut meat or freshly picked apples. If the spoilage problem could be significantly reduced or eliminated, then food could be distributed throughout the country.

Freshness was a necessity, not a luxury, so shippers began demanding something more than ventilated boxcars for moving food products, which is how produce such as vegetables and fruit was moved in the earliest days of railroading. The ventilation helped reduce spoilage, but refrigeration would be even better, allowing produce to be hauled farther. Also, items of a more perishable nature such as eggs, fish, berries, and bananas could be made available to people everywhere.

The concept of ice refrigeration predated the American railroad by a quarter of a century or so, with home refrigeration (the "ice box") coming of age at the

A trackmobile belonging to Total Logistic Control Company (formerly Rochelle Cold Storage) shuffles about the RCS grounds at Rochelle, Illinois, with two modern refrigerator cars in late summer 1998. Modern cooling and insulation methods have permitted the stocky little reefers of yore to evolve into large, high-capacity cars. *Mike Schafer*

Fresh out of the paint barn, a handsome new reefer rides the transfer table at the Chicago, Milwaukee & St. Paul's shop complex in Milwaukee, Wisconsin, in 1889. Owned by the CM&StP but carrying advertising for the Fred Miller Brewing Company, also of Milwaukee, this car will soon be hauling kegs of brew, kept cool by ice and cow-hair insulation. Note the car's link-and-pin couplers and leaf-spring archbar trucks. The car has a 15-ton capacity but has yet to be weighed for its "LT. WT." stencil. *Milwaukee Road Historical Association Archives*

dawn of the nineteenth century. Ice cut from lakes in large blocks during the winter was stored for summer use in ice sheds insulated with straw. The earliest attempts at railcar refrigeration were straightforward: blocks of ice in a boxcar. If the boxcar could somehow be better insulated to retain the cold (assuming warm-weather travel), so much the better.

By the mid-1800s there were isolated instances of insulated boxcars, with ice, transporting butter, cheese, and meat. By the end of the 1850s, the demand for refrigerated transport was spreading, and by 1860 the true refrigerator car was born—cars with heavily insulated sides, ice bunkers at either end, roof hatches for loading ice, and a drainage system for meltwater. However, these newfangled cars were still regarded as a curiosity.

Shippers were far more enthusiastic about this innovation than the railroads. The transport of dressed meat in reefers posed a serious threat to the movement of livestock. By the Civil War period, railroads had invested heavily in livestock transport and its entire associated infrastructure (stock pens and the like), and felt that the reefer would devalue those investments. Further, railroads could not afford special-purpose cars that would be used by only one shipper.

Shippers, especially meatpackers, of course, felt otherwise, and they got around the railroads' reluctance to invest in reefer fleets by building and operating their own refrigerator cars. Thus was born the private refrigerator car line, a concept that prevails to this day. By the 1870s, refrigerator cars were being built by a number of carbuilding companies for a proliferating number of new private-car lines.

Throughout the history of the refrigerator car, its overall construction dimensions paralleled that of its plain-Jane cousin, the boxcar. In the late 1880s, reefers were generally no more than 30 feet long, 10 feet wide, and 10 feet high from floor frame to roof and could carry about 20 tons of product. The 36-foot reefer then

A Pennsylvania Railroad reefer built in 1906 stands amidst shuffling switchers at the Delaware, Lackawanna & Western yards in Jersey City, New Jersey, in 1918. Though featuring steel truss underframes, most of the rest of the car is of wood construction, right down to the end ladders. *DL&W photo, Mike Del Vecchio collection, courtesy Alvin Smith*

became commonplace because loading doors at packing houses were on 36-foot centers. Meat reefers were equipped with racks and hooks so that sides of beef could be suspended from roof supports.

Techniques and materials for car cooling and insulation varied widely, however, as every builder seemed to have a different theory on how to best insulate a reefer. Initially, cars were simply iced without any kind of interior air circulation. Ice was put into the bunkers through rooftop hatches, and meltwater drained through bunker drains in the floor. Conventional wis-

dom put ice bunkers at either car end, but some cars employed overhead bunkers.

By the turn of the century, mattes of treated cattle hair had replaced sawdust, ground charcoal, or diatomaceous earth as a popular insulating material, and rubber lining on interior walls went a long way in reducing the amount of warm air that crept in through the joints of a wood wall. In 1926, Celotex (pressed fiberboard) came into use. Fiberglass gained recognition in the 1930s, but all-fiberglass insulated cars did not appear until the mid-1950s.

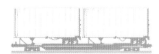

Pacific Fruit Express

Refrigerator-car companies sprang up as fast as reefers could be built. Some were successful; many weren't. Larger car companies acquired others. America's largest—and among the most well known and successful—refrigerator-car operator was the Pacific Fruit Express (PFE) Company. The brainchild of Union Pacific Chairman E. H. Harriman, who also owned a controlling interest in the Southern Pacific Lines, Pacific Fruit Express was a joint venture of UP and SP providing complete refrigerated transport *service* (cars, icing, shops, administration, and so forth) to both railroads and their subsidiaries.

PFE began in 1907 by taking over a service that had been started by Armour (of meat-packing fame) Car Lines. West Coast fruit and vegetable farming was experiencing rapid growth at this time, and there was tremendous demand for this produce in the eastern United States. Starting with 6,600 cars, the fleet gradually grew until leveling off at about 40,000 cars between 1930 and 1955. Western Pacific joined PFE in 1923, supplying cars proportional to its share of the traffic. Services were provided to other railroads as well.

One of the big reasons for PFE's success was its year-round use of railcars. Unlike other roads whose cars might be used only for a harvest that occupied a few weeks of each year, PFE's fleet "followed the sun." The cars handled potatoes in the Pacific Northwest during the autumn months, moved California's citrus during the winter, and transported spring fruit from the Southwest while northern climes were thawing out. Instead of the standard per-diem agreement (see the sidebar in chapter 1 on freight-car

movement), PFE's car hire was on a mileage basis. A rate of about four cents per mile (in 1960) was charged to the railroad whether the car was loaded or empty. The railroad then collected freight charges from the shippers according to published tariffs. PFE was paid their mileage and icing fees from this charge; the remainder was the railroad's share for handling the car. PFE's car mileage in 1960 produced gross revenues of more than $50 million.

The Depression really didn't hurt PFE—after all, people still had to buy food—but the demands of World War II did put a tremendous strain on the fleet. Many of the older reefers were completely rebuilt during this time.

The postwar 1940s and the 1950s were perhaps the best years for PFE, which peaked with a fleet of about 40,000 cars, 20 ice plants, and five shop complexes. PFE built many of its own cars, as well as purchasing

Air circulation went a long way in evening out interior temperatures, and although carbuilders experimented with fan-induced circulation as early as the late nineteenth century, they were stymied by the lack of a reliable, consistent source of power for the fans. Finally, in 1941, Pacific Fruit Express introduced a state-of-the-art circulated-air cooling system. Axle-driven alternators produced electricity for fans that forced air up through end-of-car ice bunkers and then out through vents in the car ceiling into the interior. The cooled air drifted down through contents and through grating in the floor, where it was ducted back through the bunkers via the fans. During the winters, oil heaters prevented freezing on certain items like potatoes.

Through all this, the icing station remained a fixture on the nation's railroad network. Ice melts, of course, and periodically required replacement during a reefer's journey. Icing stations, usually run by car-line companies, often were located at railroad division points where trains had to stop for crew changes and inspections. Here, reefers needing attention were switched from the train and moved to the icing racks where workers pushed blocks of ice, moving along conveyors, to and into the reefers' roof hatches. All-reefer trains—which ran on tight, fast schedules and were commonplace into the 1970s—could be brought into an icing station intact.

The postwar boom of the frozen-food industry relegated the classic iced reefer to the history books. Ice refrigeration's downfall was that it could not completely freeze contents. Optimally, frozen foods require below-zero temperatures for transport and storage—well beyond the means of ice refrigeration. Initially, railroads and car-line companies approached the problem by placing the product, prefrozen, into cars with extra-thick insulation. Ice was still employed, with the addition of salt to further lower the surrounding air temperature, but this method only worked for relatively short trips.

Enter the mechanical reefer, which dispensed with the icing process. Although there is a long history of experimentation with mechanical refrigeration, it did not come into widespread use on railroads until after World War II. Notoriously lethargic in the innovation arena, American railroads were content with ice reefers.

A new 50-foot PFE reefer stands out in a crowd of otherwise dreary-looking freight cars in a westbound Rock Island freight at Bureau, Illinois, in 1977. The emblems of Union Pacific and Southern Pacific denote PFE's joint ownership. *Mike McBride*

them from carbuilders. After the war, PFE placed the largest single order ever for reefers—5,000 cars. About a third of the refrigerator cars in the United States belonged to PFE.

PFE shipped its first carload of frozen food in 1931. This business steadily increased, with PFE carrying half of all frozen food shipped in the United States by mid-century. PFE began buying mechanical refrigerator cars in 1952 and last ordered ice reefers in 1957.

North American Despatch 6000, built in 1927, is typical of the "car line" reefers, owned and operated through lease arrangement by the car builder. At the time of this "builder's photo," this car was probably going to be leased to the Washington Co-operative Association for egg service. Fleets of these classic cars were built in the 1920s and 1930s, and many were still in service in the 1960s. Some even lasted into the 1970s still in regular service. Because they were in food service and loads tended to be far lighter than the car's 40-ton capacity, cars of this type survived well as they were maintained more regularly than a gondola or ordinary boxcar. Also, due to the seasonal nature of hauling perishables, refrigerator cars in general made far fewer loaded trips than other types of freight and tended to move loaded in one direction only. *North American Car Corporation, Mike Del Vecchio collection*

After all, the ice system worked; why go to something else? Besides, mechanical refrigeration was a relatively unproven technology, and railroads were not interested in investing in it.

Fruit Growers Express, a southeastern firm owned by the Pennsylvania Railroad, Baltimore & Ohio, and other railroads involved in the movement of oranges from Florida to the North, was first with widespread use of mechanical refrigeration, just after World War II. Initially, gasoline engines were used to directly drive the refrigeration devices, but then carbuilders took heed of the emerging diesel-electric locomotive and began using that technology: a diesel engine driving an alternator to produce electricity to power refrigeration devices.

Rather than immediately make an across-the-board switch to mechanical refrigeration, railroads and car-builders continued to use ice reefers until the end of their service life—about 25 years—which for many cars meant the 1960s.

Improvements in both mechanical refrigeration and insulation have since yielded considerably larger and more efficient refrigerator cars. On the other hand, the decentralization of meat processing coupled with the American railroads' shift away from short-haul operations has surrendered a considerable amount of perishable traffic to trucking companies. Today, modern refrigerator cars still roll across America as interesting exceptions to the rule of TOFC (trailer-on-flatcar), container, and unit coal trains that dominate the rails. However, reefer traffic is on the rise as trucking companies find it more difficult to recruit cross-country drivers for perishable traffic.

Swift No. 25009, an early mechanical reefer, being switched on the Whitewater Valley Railroad, a tourist/museum line in southeastern Indiana, in 1975. The car was built in 1954 during the infancy of mechanical refrigeration in transportation. *Mike Schafer*

Back in the late 1940s when labor was cheap, seven workers load fresh tomatoes into a ventilated refrigerator car belonging to the Southern Refrigerator Car Company, owned in part by the Illinois Central. *IC, Mike Del Vecchio collection*

Santa Fe reefer 2030 was but a few weeks old when photographed on March 10, 1956. The "MTC" on the "ice"-themed door refers to "Mechanical Temperature Control." Santa Fe has devoted half the car's side to touting its famous all-Pullman *Super Chief* streamliner. *John Dziobko*

Almost 32 years after the photo at right was taken, new Santa Fe MTC reefers undergo testing at Santa Fe's huge shop complex at Topeka, Kansas, in June 1988. Even though Santa Fe had by this time been out of the passenger-train business for 17 years, the cars wear the "Ship and Travel Santa Fe All the Way" slogan. *Forrest L. Becht*

At Pennsylvania Railroad's Enola Yard in Harrisburg, Pennsylvania, in July 1955, Santa Fe and Pacific Fruit Express reefers receive special handling from a 2-10-0 locomotive. Possibly, the cars have just arrived from the West and are being moved to or from icing facilities for a quick re-icing before continuing eastward on another train. Santa Fe's reefer operation was a direct competitor to PFE. *John Dziobko*

Wood-sheathed reefers lasted well into the second half of the twentieth century, as revealed in this scene of a Western Refrigerator Lines (owned by the Green Bay & Western Railroad) car westbound on the Erie Lackawanna at State Line Tower, Hammond, Indiana, in 1965. *Mike Schafer*

A hopper car is really a sort of sophisticated gondola. The difference is that the entire floor area of a hopper is sloped toward "wells" (hoppers), which help funnel the material to the bottom hatches through which the commodity is unloaded. The hopper was critical in the development of the American railroad, for the railroad was (and still is) best at hauling huge quantities of bulk material like coal, aggregate, and grain. Coal was at one time especially important. In 1900, for example, American railroads hauled more than 300 million tons of coal alone, compared to 76 million tons of lumber, some 80 million tons of grain products, about 50 million tons of metal, and about 43 million tons of merchandise.

An ancient ancestor of the hopper was the coal jimmie, a small, four-wheel, open-top wooden car that could be unloaded through a hinged side or bottom hatch. Some had sloped interior walls to facilitate unloading—a hallmark of true hopper cars. Jimmies could be found on the pioneering railroads of America in the late 1820s and early 1830s, notably the Delaware & Hudson Canal Company and Mauch Chunk lines mentioned in chapter 1, and they each carried about two tons of coal. By about 1840 the jimmy had evolved into (although not entirely supplanted by) larger, two-truck, eight-wheel cars with a more sophisticated hopper/hatch system and more than double the carrying capacity. The hopper car was born.

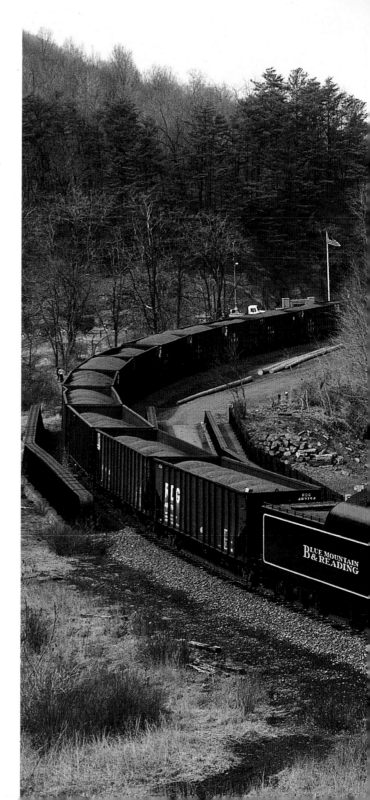

Former Reading Lines 4-8-4 No. 2102 has a grip on a hopper train slogging over the Blue Mountain & Reading Railroad in eastern Pennsylvania in the spring of 1991. The restored steam locomotive is making a guest appearance on the shortline, which operates portions of former Reading trackage. Reading predecessor Philadelphia & Reading was one of the nation's first railroads to own and operate a large fleet of hopper cars for coal service. *Jim Boyd*

Despite the early appearance of the hopper, it did not rapidly catch on, and jimmies remained popular with the railroads well into the late 1800s, finally dying out by 1900. Meanwhile, many railroads were using drop- or hopper-bottom gondolas, especially those roads that did not have enough year-round mineral traffic to warrant true hoppers. Drop- or hopper-bottom gondolas could be used to haul nonbulk commodities such as lumber or crated merchandise when coal traffic was down.

The true hopper can only haul substances that can self-unload by way of the car's sloped sides, hoppers, and hatches, so initially hoppers were found primarily on railroads where mineral traffic was the primary reason for their existence. One of these was the Philadelphia & Reading, a Pennsylvania coal-country predecessor of the Reading Railroad (of Monopoly game fame), which boasted a fleet of 10-ton-capacity

Wooden hoppers belonging to the Chicago & North Western Railway early in the twentieth century haul crushed stone that is probably being used to ballast C&NW track. *Mike McBride* collection

Bessemer & Lake Erie 43604 was built in 1918 by American Car & Foundry at Berwyck, Pennsylvania. The "U.S." lettering indicates this and its sister cars were ordered under the United States Railroad Administration, which operated most of the nation's railroads during World War II; the car is a standard 55-ton hopper of USRA design. B&LE ancestor Pittsburgh, Bessemer & Lake Erie was a pioneer in all-steel car construction, operating a test fleet of steel hoppers at the close of the nineteenth century. *Mike Del Vecchio collection*

Aluminum construction for hoppers (or any type of freight car, for that matter) was not widely accepted until the 1970s, although instances of aluminum cars long predate that. This aluminum hopper was built by Alcoa Aluminum in 1931 and is shown nicely refurbished and on display in August 1998 outside the Ward Stone Company near Monon, Indiana. The markings on the side proclaim this to be "The only all-aluminum open top hopper built in the United States," a statement that was perhaps true for the first 40 years or so of its life. The car sports the livery of the Monon Railroad, which once served the stone plant. *Mike Schafer*

wooden hoppers in the mid-1800s. Later in the century, the P&R acquired hoppers that doubled that capacity and, as the nineteenth century wound down, was operating thousands of hoppers. P&R appeared to be one of the earliest railroads to embrace the hopper on a widespread basis, but the cars quickly caught on with other coal-hauling railroads.

By the late 1800s, hopper capacity had reached 30-40 tons, thanks in part to the increased use of metal parts that made for stronger cars. The number of hopper bays would eventually be used to designate hopper cars. A "twin" hopper had two bays, a "triple" had three, and a "quad" had four. The type of hopper purchased was determined not by the number of bays, however, but by the car's carrying capacity. Larger hoppers had more bays simply

because there was more room for them, and more bays allowed for faster unloading.

Thanks largely to the reign of the coal industry, the multibay open-top hopper became a prominent fixture on American railroads—particularly those serving the coalfields of the Northeast, Southeast, and Midwest. (In 1960, for example, Norfolk & Western's freight-car fleet of 77,044 cars included 59,574 hoppers.) During the first half of the twentieth century, coal was universally used to warm and power America, from the countless coal-fired stoves and furnaces found in nearly every American home to the huge power plants that generated electricity to light homes and businesses. Further, the railroad industry itself consumed huge quantities of coal to power its steam locomotives. Hoppers also hauled coke (a processed coal,

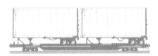

Ore Jennies

Iron ore can be hauled in a conventional hopper, but because the material is considerably more dense than coal, only a relatively small volume can be loaded before the car's capacity is breached. For this reason, there are hoppers specifically designed for handling ore, and they are widely known as "jennies." The have the same overall format as a conventional hopper—sloping floor, hopper wells, and hatches—but are of considerably shorter height and length. In addition, the floor slopes are of greater pitch, as ore does not slide out of the car as easily as coal or coke. (This problem has in part been allevi-ated by the introduction of taconite, ore mixed with bentonite clay and made into pellets.)

Although the first ore jennies probably date from about the mid-1800s, not until the domestic rise of iron production late in that century did jennies come into widespread use on those railroads serving ore-mining regions and steel mills. Railroads owning a high proportion of ore jennies included the Duluth, Missabe & Iron Range; Chicago & North Western; Bessemer & Lake Erie; Milwaukee Road; Duluth, South Shore & Atlantic; and Soo Line.

It might be short and stubby, but this little ore jenny is loaded with more than 75 tons of taconite pellets. The car, photographed in 1988, belongs to the king of ore-hauling United States railroads, the Duluth, Missabe & Iron Range. *James Mischke*

Chesapeake & Ohio 53048 illustrates the return to composite construction during World War II as a means of conserving plate steel. Built in August 1943 by Pullman-Standard, the car had a 50-ton capacity. *Pullman-Standard, Mike Del Vecchio collection*

lighter and cleaner-burning) to fuel furnaces at foundries and steel mills.

After World War II, "king coal" was dethroned. In 1960, the last steam locomotive in mainline service fell to the diesel-electric locomotive that had quietly entered the railroad scene some 30 years earlier. Petroleum was the new king, and it was being used to heat homes and businesses—and fuel diesel locomotives, too. Domestic steel manufacturing declined as offshore steel plants wooed customers with lower prices, further reducing the need for coal and coke movement. Growing environmental concerns cast a pall over the soft-coal industry as many power plants were required to shift to low-sulfur coal, found mainly in the American West.

Beginning in the 1970s, the low-sulfur end of the coal industry has enjoyed an unprecedented boom, and unit-coal trains flowing out of Wyoming and Montana to power plants throughout the United States are today a common sight. However, much of this coal moves in rotary-dump cars that technically are gondolas. Instead, the reign of the hopper car has diverged, and today the *covered* hopper, in its many forms, has become prominent.

Covered Hoppers

Railroads love to move coal, stone, coke, and iron-ore pellets. These commodities can move in open-top cars, and they won't complain about rain, sleet, snow, or heat of summer day—nor will such weather extremes seriously affect their loading or unloading. This is not true of all hopper ladings, however. An open-top hopper of grain that gets rained on and then rolls out across the prairies under hot summer sun will quickly start on its way to becoming the world's largest bread loaf. Similarly, an open hopper of cement passing through a rainstorm would quickly turn into the world's largest paperweight—on wheels.

Although well suited to the self-unloading attribute of hoppers, such commodities need to be protected from the elements, and so the covered hopper was born. Crude covered hoppers appeared in the 1830s for purposes of moving grain. These ancient covered hoppers had lift-up top covers for loading and bottom hatches for unloading. Regardless of the obvious advantages to this design, the covered-hopper concept did not catch on as quickly as one might expect, and—outfitted with special grain doors—the *boxcar* became widely used for grain movement during the late nineteenth century and throughout the first half of

Different hoppers, same job—hauling coal. Different styles of hoppers line up at an unknown location along the Pennsylvania Railroad in July 1956. Baltimore & Ohio 636210 is a 37-foot hopper with a 50-ton capacity; PRR 267917 is a 46-foot car with a 70-ton capacity, while its mate is a 44-foot car with the same capacity. Note the round-top "shields" on the ends of the Chesapeake & Ohio hopper beyond, a design element used to reduce spill over the ends during hard starts and stops. *John Dziobko*

the twentieth century. Meanwhile, the covered hopper fared better in the movement of lime, cement, dry sand (sand that got wet while being hauled in open-top hoppers could be easily dried, but covered hoppers reduced the need for sand-drying equipment), and other similar materials that required protection from moisture.

In time, hinged roof covers gave way to permanent roofs outfitted with square or round locking hatches. Covered hoppers have floor sides more steeply sloped

than their open-top counterparts to help dense material like cement and sand flow better out the bottom hatches. Cars assigned to sand and cement service tend to be smaller than their coal-hauling open-top counterparts because of the density and weight of those materials.

The use of covered hoppers for grain did not accelerate much until after World War II in general and during the late 1960s and 1970s in particular. Although freight traffic—and subsequently car fleets—was declining overall

Lehigh New England 12778 is typical of the short all-steel covered hoppers of the mid-twentieth century. The 29-foot car, shown restored in 1996 at Big Moose Lake, New York, had a 70-ton capacity. Based in eastern Pennsylvania and western New Jersey, the LNE hauled a considerable amount of cement until being mostly abandoned in 1961, with the Jersey Central taking over portions of the line. *Mike Schafer*

after the war, on some railroads the covered hopper was the only type of car whose numbers were increasing. The arrival of the "jumbo" covered hopper—cars with a capacity of 70-100 tons or more—was just what railroads were waiting for. More grain could be hauled in a jumbo than in a 40-foot grain boxcar, and they were easier to load and unload thanks to state-of-the-art car mechanisms. Cylindrical all-steel covered hoppers were the next step, allowing for yet more capacity and a stronger, airtight car in which air pressure itself could be applied to facilitate unloading.

Today, grain (including corn) movement is the most common use of covered hoppers, which themselves have become one of the most popular types of freight cars found on today's railroads. Other commodities commonly handled in covered hoppers include flour, plastic pellets, potash (a fertilizer), fishmeal, and soybeans. In America's breadbasket, the unit grain train has become a ritual of the postharvest season, and the covered hopper plays a key role in feeding the nation.

Cylindrical, welded steel hoppers make for an exceptionally strong, lightweight car with added capacity. This new CSX hopper at Connersville, Indiana, in 1996 can carry well over 110 tons of grain. *Bradley McClelland*

Covered hoppers receive their payload at a Farmers' Co-op grain facility at Moweaqua, Illinois, on the Decatur Junction Railway in July 1991. *Howard Ande*

Colorful Illinois Terminal, known for its lime-green and yellow diesel locomotives, had equally colorful freight equipment, as attested by new (1975) IT covered hoppers rolling west on a Penn Central train at Marion, Ohio. ITC 2038 illustrates the 100-ton covered hopper that had found great favor among farm-belt railroads. Formerly an electric interurban railroad serving central and south-central Illinois, IT was entrenched in some of the best agricultural land in the country and moved grain and grain products more than any other commodity. *David P. Oroszi*

7 | Tank Cars

Traditionally resistant to change and innovation, except when it saved them money, railroads would probably have forever hauled all freight in either boxcars or gons had the matter been entirely up to them. Indeed, in the early days of railroading this even applied to liquid commodities—molasses, whale oil (for lamps), and vinegar, for example—in which case it was put into barrels for shipment in a gon or boxcar.

The tank car was a late bloomer in the pages of freight-car history, not becoming commonplace until well after the Civil War. Tank-car development was spurred by the infant petroleum industry, which got its start in the late 1850s in northwestern Pennsylvania thanks to Edwin Drake, who showed that it was possible to extract oil from the ground in large quantities. The oil industry boomed in the 1860s and designs for "oil" (tank) cars began to emerge during that same decade while crude oil was being shipped via traditional methods—in barrels in gons, boxcars, or stockcars. Railroads, of course, were happy with this arrangement, but oil shippers did not like the expense and vulnerability of barrels, which could be easily damaged or stolen.

The earliest "tank" cars of the 1860s were simply flatcars outfitted with wooden vats. The flaws of this design quickly became obvious: the vats couldn't be wider than the flatcar, and their height was limited as well; wood-slatted sides held together by iron straps were vulnerable to car movement and prone to leaks. By the end of the 1860s, this top-heavy design had been supplanted by a longitudinal iron tank mounted on a flatcar or similar platform, although existing vat-type cars continued in service for several years. Cars of this new format featured a top dome for expansion and usually included a safety valve; a discharge valve was

A westbound quartet of Southern Pacific locomotives rolls a string of tank cars into the sunset at Soledad Canyon, California, in 1988. *Mike Del Vecchio*

In the early 1900s, wooden tank cars were used to transport such items as vinegar and spring water. The tanks were built with staves and steel bands, much like a barrel. This car, built by Chicago, Milwaukee & St. Paul's Milwaukee Shops in June 1910, will carry water ("Corrins Waukesha Water" is barely visible on the upper side of the car) for Hinckley & Schmitt, a water distributor still in business today. Some features of cars from this era include truss rods and outside-hung brake beams on the light archbar trucks. This car's rated capacity is 19 tons—not much by today's standards. Although a few cars of this type survived in regular service into the early 1970s (though equipped with modern trucks, couplers, and braking equipment), most were long ago replaced by cars with glass-lined steel tanks. *Milwaukee Road Historical Association archives*

located on the car's underbelly. They could carry about 3,400 gallons (about 80 barrels), but this capacity would soon begin to increase, reaching as much as 8,000 gallons by the turn of the century. The early cars were about 28 feet long.

Once established, the traditional tank car gained wide acceptance during the 1870s and 1880s, especially by the burgeoning oil industry, but by the turn of the century, the tank car was being used to transport any number of liquid commodities including water, milk, fruit juice, paint, and turpentine. In the 1890s, the steel tank began replacing the iron tank, and during the same period, the all-steel underframe tank car appeared.

As with the refrigerator car, railroads were hesitant to invest in tank cars. Unlike flatcars, gondolas, boxcars, and even stockcars, tank cars spent half their transit time empty. Once they reached their destination, they were unloaded and had to return to home base empty. With boxcars and such, there was always a chance of "backhaul" whereby the car, once emptied, could be commandeered by the local freight agent and loaded with something else for the trip back home (see the sidebar on car movement in chapter 1). However, a tank car that had been brimming with oil could not be returned loaded with wine, fruit juice, or just about anything else, for that matter, except more oil.

As far as early oil company tank cars went, SRDX 410 was a big one at 10,000-gallon capacity. Most of these cars tended to be 8,000 gallons or smaller. At first glance, tank cars tended to be rather look-alike, probably due to the fact they almost always were painted black. But there was a lot of variation in tank and dome size and construction (note the heavily riveted seams) as well as other details. This car was built in November 1913 and was almost certainly in regular service right up to 1956 when its Andrews-style trucks were outlawed for interchange service. The car is shown at Bolton, Missouri, in 1993. *Gerald A. Hook*

Fairly small as tank cars go, ACFX 481 appears to be a 4,000-gallon car with a welded tank for chemical service. Generally, cars in chemical service had a walkway built around the dome. This early car was built by American Car & Foundry, which also operates it. Note the car's "tight-lock" couplers, which feature a design that helps keep cars coupled (and therefore more likely upright) in the event of a derailment. This lessens the possibility of the tank becoming punctured by the other cars' couplers. The car is shown at Columbus, Ohio, in 1983. *Bradley McClelland*

Regardless of their inherent drawback, tank cars were in high demand by oil companies, and—as with the refrigerator car—many purchased their own tank-car fleets rather than relying on the railroads to supply cars. Similarly, car-line companies were formed to operate tank-car fleets, leasing cars to customers, although during railroading's notorious "rail baron" era of the late 1800s, some oil magnates—for example, John D. Rockefeller and his Union Tank Car Line—attempted to monopolize tank-car operations, and the government had to intervene.

The stunning rise of the automobile early in the twentieth century resulted in the erosion of rail passenger service, but it proved a boon for freight traffic as demand for petroleum products—and therefore tank cars—exploded. The variety of other liquid products shipped by rail was increasing as well: chemicals (such as chlorine and ammonia) and cleaning acids, edible oils as well as oils used for furniture finishing, paints and stains, and kaolin, a fine-grained clay in semiliquid form used in the manufacture of glassware. In addition, the crude oil that had become a staple of tank-car lading was being refined into an amazing variety of products: gasoline, motor oil, distillate (lightly refined gasoline), kerosene, and eventually diesel fuel. Milk was moved in special glass-lined tank cars, usually on expedited schedules and often on passenger trains.

Carbuilders cranked out new tank cars by the thousands, with American Car & Foundry and General American becoming the leading manufacturers of tank cars. By 1930, well over 100,000 tank cars were shuttling about America, loaded with more than 100 different types of liquid commodities. The expansion of tank car use was interrupted by the Great Depression, and the national fleet declined by several thousand cars by the end of the 1930s. The slump would prove short-lived, as the tank car would be critical to America's victory in World War II. When German submarines in the Atlantic began sinking tanker ships bound for the United States, the railroads and tank-car companies took over, using new tank-car fleets to distribute oil that had arrived on the West Coast.

After the war, pipelines and trucking began to make inroads on the railroads' share of liquid transportation, but this was offset somewhat by a continuing increase in the variety of ladings carried in tank cars. For example, in the 1960s and 1970s, corn syrup began to replace cane sugar in food production, and the tank car was called upon to handle the boom in syrup transport.

As the 1950s got under way, tank-car construction was improved through all-welded (versus riveted) tanks and an increased use of aluminum. These and other technological improvements, such as high-pressure tanks that eliminated the dome, allowed railroads to carry larger quantities of liquids per car and undercut the costs of trucking.

A Conrail-owned "trackmobile" still carrying Penn Central markings shuffles tank cars about in the fall of 1978 on the once-extensive array of industrial street trackage that once webbed the harborfront areas of Baltimore, Maryland. *Mike Schafer*

Kanotex 879 is an early 8,000-gallon car with the tanks divided into three compartments, hence the three domes. Cars of this type could be used to transport smaller amounts of different liquids. They weren't very common and tended to be custom-designed and built for a fairly specific service. Many, as in this case, were owned by the company whose products they carried. Depending on the need, some were built with only two domes and compartments, or as many as six. Shown at Galveston, Texas, in 1989, this is an interesting car with its silver paint, large lettering, and an array of domes and ladders. *Tom Kline*

Built in 1960 when tank cars tended to be rather drab, UTLX 59137 looks quite dapper in the bright red and black colors of Union Starch Company of Granite City, Illinois. Often cars that are on a long-term lease would be painted up for the lessee. Note the walkway around the small dome. On most cars, dome size was required to be a minimum of two percent of tank volume. *Hank Goerke*

Dupont 29728 can carry 43,800 gallons and is in assigned service at New Orleans in 1988. The extreme weight of this car when loaded requires the double-truck arrangement. Note that the tank rests on a bolster that spans each truck pair. Of special interest on this car are its end ladders, side walkway, and offset dome. The unloading valve on the frameless car can easily be seen. Because of their size and weight, these cars are restricted from general interchange service. *Gerald A. Hook*

8   Special-Service Cars

The common thread among the types of freight cars covered in the previous chapters is that each can carry any variety of products. Generally, special-service cars carry a specific type of freight. Their design is such that it would be impractical to use the car to haul anything other than its intended freight.

Auto-Carriers

Automobiles and other road vehicles being transported by rail from factory to showroom used to move almost exclusively in auto boxcars. Although boxcars served as nice little rolling garages, protecting the shiny new vehicles from the elements, they were not particularly efficient for the job because they were awkward to load and were limited in the number of autos they could hold.

After World War II, the trucking industry began to boom, thanks in part to improved highways and—beginning in the mid-1950s—the coming of the Interstate. Tractor-hauled rigs specially designed to handle as many automobiles as a boxcar—about a half dozen autos—nearly wiped out the railroad's finished-auto traffic.

What the railroads needed were railcars on which vehicles could easily be loaded—a high number of them, thereby undercutting trucking rates. Although a large, high-cube boxcar could certainly be modified to accomplish this, railroads wanted to keep the railcar's weight at a minimum. The weight of a boxcar's sides and ends alone can quickly add up, reducing the capacity for vehicles. In addition, vehicles themselves were

Trains of well cars and modern enclosed auto-racks pass each other on the Santa Fe at Sheffield interlocking in Kansas City, Missouri, in March 1996. Such special-service cars were commonplace on the nation's main lines by this time, but only 35 years earlier the auto-rack was still a curiosity and the stack or well car unheard of. *Dan Munson*

Today's automobile carrier cars are known as auto-racks, an apt description and a common sight on today's railroads. A far cry from the old double-door automobile boxcars of the 1940s and 1950s, these cars have greater capacity and can be loaded and unloaded much faster. The cars are configured in double and triple decks as needed. These cars were first built with open sides and no roofs, like this triple-deck CP Rail car carrying 18 new autos at Middletown, Ohio, in 1988. *Brad McClelland*

Because of increasing vandalism, newer auto-racks were built with protective panels on their sides while many older open cars, such as this TrailerTrain auto-rack assigned to the Frisco, were retrofitted with panels. The panels used today are made of sheet metal, perforated to let light into the cavernous interior and reduce weight. Most new auto-racks—such as those appearing in the opening photo of this chapter—are built with roofs, covered sides, and end doors. This load of Ford Pintos is eastbound on a Norfolk & Western freight out of Kansas City in March 1971. *Forrest L. Becht*

changing. For decades, manufacturers determined overall auto size specifications based on the number of autos that could efficiently fit into a railroad boxcar. The more cars that could fit into a car, the lower the per-auto shipping costs. But, by the late 1950s, consumers were demanding ever-larger cars, and manufacturers were responding by manufacturing ever-larger cars—at the same time shifting the onus of the resultant shipping problems to the transportation companies: "We're the customer. We've got a product to ship; *you* figure out how best to do it at a good price for us!"

The answer was not to triple-deck or further lengthen a boxcar, but to double-or triple-deck and lengthen a *flatcar*. Presto! The auto-rack was born. Each 89-foot bi-level car could carry 8-10 standard-size autos while tri-level racks could carry 12-15 autos. Trailer-Train Corporation, the 1950s pioneers of TOFC transport, also became a pioneer of auto-rack development in the late 1950s. Soon, the auto-rack caught on and began turning up everywhere. Some railroads, such as the Santa Fe, were building their own, using cushioned-underframed flatcars as a foundation.

Regardless of the builder, the overall format was the same. Automobiles were simply driven onto auto-racks and parked, nose-to-tail, elephant-style. Multiple, coupled auto-racks could be loaded just as easily, thanks to drop steps connecting the driveways of each level. The only flaw in the design of first-generation auto-racks was that they were completely open, making the shiny new vehicles tempting targets for trackside rock-throwers—or comfortable places for hoboes to snooze while hitching a ride. Soon, railroad shop forces were bolting side panels to the auto-racks to shield their cargo, while the next generation of auto-racks came fully enclosed with tops and sides of lightweight sheet metal and lockable end doors.

A short-lived but interesting auto-carrier deserves mention: the "Vert-A-Pac" cars that made a flash-in-the-pan appearance in the 1970s. The impetus for this unusual railcar was Chevrolet's Vega, a subcompact auto designed to compete head-to-head with Volkswagen's popular Beetle.

Keeping the Vega's sticker price low involved several strategies, one of which was the reduction of transportation costs. The Vert-A-Pac railcar was the solution here, and it represented a radical departure from conventional auto transport methods: Each Vert-A-Pac car carried a record 30 autos—vertically! As an aluminum-engined, low-profile car, Vegas didn't take up much room nor did they weigh much, so standing (hanging, actually) them on end proved practical.

Stack (Well) Cars

When containerization finally caught on in a widespread basis in North America in the 1980s, the need for a special railcar to efficiently carry containers grew urgent. Although containers could be hauled on standard flatcars with relative ease, they could not be carried in sufficient numbers to make the traffic worthwhile to the railroads. Further, the use of standard flatcars required that containers be tied down, which hampered quick loading and unloading.

One of the most unusual of the auto-carrying cars was the Vert-A-Pac. Built to haul Chevrolet Vegas, the sides of this car comprised fold-down hatches. Each Vega was backed onto the cranked-down side compartment, secured, and then cranked back up like a Murphy bed, storing the car vertically. A vertical row of 15 autos could be carried on each side—30 cars total per car—in this manner. Southern Pacific Vert-A-Pac 517139 is at Dallas, Texas, in 1976. *Gerald A. Hook*

Looking like something out of a Jules Verne novel is the bottle car. Like a huge thermos bottle on wheels, these cars transport molten steel from furnace to mill. Used in comparatively short, captive-service runs, these cars are obviously not in regular interchange service. When loaded through a domelike opening with molten steel, the tanks—or bottles—can be turned over to dump the steel out at the mill. These cars are being loaded at the blast furnace at Bethlehem Steel in Bethlehem, Pennsylvania, in 1995. *Mike Del Vecchio*

The articulated spine car was designed for piggyback truck-trailer transport. Unlike a conventional flatcar, the spine car's deck is not continuous. It only needs to support the back wheels of the trailer because they are loaded and unloaded by overhead cranes—not by driving the trailers on and off the car. Some spine cars are articulated; that is, they are sectionalized in as many as five segments, with each section sharing a common truck, thereby reducing weight and maintenance costs. These spine cars are rolling along Conrail's Pittsburgh-Harrisburg main line at Horseshoe Curve, Pennsylvania, in 1994. *Tom Kline*

Containers themselves had become standardized such that they could be stacked and interlocked one upon the other. Unfortunately, two containers stacked were too high for railroads to handle, not only because of bridge and tunnel clearances, but because double-stacked containers on standard flatcars had a dangerously high center of gravity.

The answer was to cross a gondola with a depressed-center flatcar. The result was a "well" car—a depressed-center flatcar with low sides. One container can fit neatly into the well area with another resting on top. The depressed center lowers the overall height of the loads and at the same time lowers the center of gravity. The containers are easily loaded or unloaded with an overhead crane.

Efficiency was taken one step farther with the introduction of the "articulated" well or stack car, which can carry 10 containers. The articulated—or jointed—car features five sections (two containers per section), with each section sharing a single truck with the adjacent section. What appears to be five stack cars is really considered by the owning railroad or car company to be a single car—with 24 wheels! Watch any stack train go by and you'll likely see a combination of single and articulated stack cars, with perhaps an occasional piggyback flat thrown in carrying a container or two, but only single level.

These specially built Union Pacific cars are hauling aircraft subassemblies in a Rock Island freight at Ottawa, Illinois, in June 1976. Spotting these special-service cars in their myriad configurations is part of what makes train-watching fun. *Mike McBride*

With their articulated and multiple-car sets, well cars were constructed to the same economic parameters as the spine cars. These cars have a low-slung body and special bulkheads and tie-downs to carry two standard shipping containers, one atop the other. Despite the depressed-center design of these cars (to lower the center of gravity and provide overhead clearance), loaded double-stack cars are still very tall and are restricted from service on some lines. These Twin-Stack cars at Portland, Oregon, in 1988 have just been delivered from their builder. A view of loaded well cars can be seen at the end of chapter 1. *Mike Schafer*

Other Special-Service Cars

The auto-carrier and the well car are among the most common special-service cars, but examples of other railcars of this league abound. A few are noted or illustrated here.

The "spine" car represents another step in the evolution of the TOFC flatcar. As the name implies, the spine car is little more than a center sill on trucks. One end has minimal platforms for supporting trailer wheels, while the other carries the "fifth wheel" for supporting the nonwheeled end of a tractor trailer. The principal drawback in hauling trailers is that much of what is being hauled is "dead weight" in the form of the trailer's wheel assemblies and tires. Spine-car design in part tackles the problem by reducing the weight of the railcar itself, with some mounted on four wheels instead of the usual double trucks. Some spine cars are articulated in as many as five sections and can handle up to five trailers. Spine cars can also carry containers.

"Bottle" cars are particularly interesting, although their ranks are small and their range is isolated. They are comprised of ponderously heavy, insulated steel tanks that carry molten steel or slag. The tanks themselves are self-supporting—there is no center sill or other framework—with each end supported by a set of double trucks, necessary for the extreme weight of a loaded car. Often, gons are used to separate bottle cars in transit to spread out the weight of the train, which moves (at restricted speeds) molten metal between blast-furnace complexes and steel-forging and fabrication plants, which might be several miles away. Discharge is accomplished by rotating the tank of the bottle car.

The above are just a few of the numerous cars designed for special service. Others could fill a whole book unto themselves.

Index